Heritage Places

of Singapore

WAN MENG HAO
JACQUELINE LAU

Marshall Cavendish
Editions

Title block for chapter openers © Debbie Schiel/Stock.xchng
Parchment for chapter openers and scroll for box stories © Stock.xchng

© 2009 Marshall Cavendish International (Asia) Private Limited

Senior Editor: Melvin Neo
Editor: Shawn Wee
Designer: Bernard Go Kwang Meng

Published by Marshall Cavendish Editions
An imprint of Marshall Cavendish International
1 New Industrial Road, Singapore 536196

Other Marshall Cavendish Offices
Marshall Cavendish Ltd. 5th Floor 32–38 Saffron Hill, London EC1N 8FH • Marshall Cavendish Corporation. 99 White Plains Road, Tarrytown NY 10591-9001, USA • Marshall Cavendish International (Thailand) Co Ltd. 253 Asoke, 12th Flr, Sukhumvit 21 Road, Klongtoey Nua, Wattana, Bangkok 10110, Thailand • Marshall Cavendish (Malaysia) Sdn Bhd, Times Subang, Lot 46, Subang Hi-Tech Industrial Park, Batu Tiga, 40000 Shah Alam, Selangor Darul Ehsan, Malaysia

Marshall Cavendish is a trademark of Times Publishing Limited

National Library Board Singapore Cataloguing in Publication Data
Wan, Meng Hao.
Heritage places of Singapore / Wan Meng Hao, Jacqueline Lau. – Singapore : Marshall Cavendish Editions, c2009.
p. cm.
Includes index.
ISBN-13 : 978-981-261-858-0 (pbk.)
1. Historic buildings – Singapore. 2. Historic sites – Singapore.
3. Singapore – History. I. Lau, Jacqueline. II. Title.

DS609.3
959.57 — dc22   OCN436103940

Printed in Singapore by KWF Printing Co Pte Ltd

DEDICATION
To all the global souls of the world.

CONTENTS

AUTHORS' PREFACE

People these days want a lot, and they want it quick. Although we do not believe that such behaviour, commercialism and materialism constitute the character of Singapore (we believe Singapore holds much, much more than that), we do think that having it all beautifully and conveniently laid out in one book would make it easier for someone to appreciate our rich and diversified cultural, historical and natural heritage.

Although we were both born in Hong Kong, many of our formative years were lived out in Singapore. The sense of detachment and rootlessness has perhaps led us to bear a greater inquisitiveness of any new and strange place we find ourselves in. In our own way, we have acquired insights into this environment constituting our new home and affections of the fragile charms of this tiny island. For starters, few are aware that in this highly-urbanised country, there is still rich biodiversity to be found. Or that Singapore has a pre-history as Temasek predating the arrival of Sir Stamford Raffles in 1819 by a few centuries. The excavation of archaeological artifacts from various sites have demonstrated the continuous presence of peoples from Java, Sumatra, China, India, Portugal and other regions since the Sung Dynasty.

We make no claim to cover the full richness of this island's landscape, for we merely wish to share the highlights that we perceive to be special. In addition to photographs and write-ups on each local place of interest, we've also attempted to incorporate some historical information to link the past to the present. This book maps out the island by region and contextualises it within a historical and cultural setting.

If growing up here hasn't brought us any closer to Singapore, at least this book did. We hope it will do the same for you too, be you a citizen, resident or curious visitor.

We hope you will have a great time scouting out these places in Singapore! Happy Exploring!

Wan Meng Hao
Jacqueline Lau

BRIDGES AT SINGAPORE RIVER

The Singapore River was the main economic engine of Singapore's growth as a free port for over 150 years, and its upcoming new role will see it become a provider of drinking water, with the river soon to be a part of the Marina Barrage to provide a reservoir of fresh water for Singapore.

Significant landmarks that characterise Singapore River are the various bridges that span across different sections of this 3 km-long river. These bridges include the Anderson Bridge, Cavenagh Bridge, Elgin Bridge, Ord Bridge and Read Bridge.

Anderson Bridge

Located at the mouth of the Singapore River on the banks of Empress Place and Collyer Quay, this bridge was built between 1908 and 1910 by the Public Works Department. Named in honour of Sir John Anderson, Governor of the Straits Settlements from 1904 to 1911, this bridge was constructed to handle the increased pedestrian and vehicular traffic in this part of town, and to relieve pressure off the existing Cavenagh Bridge.

Anderson Bridge

The bridge was designed by Municipal Engineer Robert Pierce and his assistant D.M. Martin. Construction of the steel bridge was carried out by Howarth Erskine Ltd, while Westminister Construction Company Ltd handled the bridging foundations and abutments, all at a total cost of $50,000.

Since its official opening on 12 March 1910, Anderson Bridge has been serving pedestrians and vehicles for close to a century.

Cavenagh Bridge

Built in 1869, Cavenagh Bridge is Singapore's oldest bridge that retains its original architecture and form. Named after Major-General Sir William Orfeur Cavenagh, the last Governor of Singapore (1859–1867) before it became a Crown Colony, this steel suspension bridge was constructed as a pedestrian footbridge. The steel structure of this bridge was fabricated in Glasgow, Scotland and assembled in Singapore. It is believed that Indian convict labour was employed in its construction.

Cavenagh Bridge

There was a flaw in the bridge's design that was overlooked in its construction, resulting in limitations of its use. It was built without consideration of the boats that plied the river transporting goods. At high tides, boats could not pass safely under the bridge as little height allowances were available, and boats laden with goods could only pass under the bridge at low tides.

The 19th century planners of Cavenagh Bridge also did not anticipate the appearance of the automobile at the turn of the 20th century. When cars appeared on the roads, it soon became clear that this bridge could not support the weight load of these modern vehicles. Hence, a new bridge (Anderson Bridge) was constructed in 1910 to meet these new needs, and Cavenagh Bridge became an exclusive pedestrian bridge. To this day, police notices on site continue to inform the public that the bridge is off limits to ox-carts, horse carriages or any other vehicles exceeding a laden weight of 3 cwt (centum weight)!

Cavenagh Bridge

Cavenagh Bridge

Elgin Bridge

The Elgin Bridge was constructed in 1929, and named after the Governor General of India James Bruce, the 8th Earl of Elgin (1862–1863). It replaced an earlier iron bridge also of the same name. Its location is historically significant, as this was where the first bridge to link both banks of Singapore River was constructed (giving rise to North and South Bridge Roads). Previous bridges on this site included the Presentment Bridge and Thomson Bridge.

Elgin Bridge is made up of concrete with steel frames. It is decorated with cast iron lamps, and complemented with bronze plaques featuring a lion standing in front of a palm tree, representing Singapura—The Lion City. These plaques are the works of the Italian sculptor Cavalori Rudolfo Nolli.

Elgin Bridge

Ord Bridge

The Ord Bridge, constructed in 1886, was named in honour of Sir Harry St. George Ord, first Governor of the Straits Settlements (1867–1873). The bridge connected River Valley Road with Magazine Road, where the British Army had set up ammunition and weapons stores in the early days of Singapore as a British settlement.

Ord's major contribution to Singapore was the commissioning of the construction of Government House at Orchard Road. This building is now known as the Istana.

Ord Bridge

Read Bridge

Read Bridge

Erected in 1887, Read Bridge was named after a prominent Scottish merchant and member of the Legislative Council, William Henry Macleod Read. This bridge replaced Merchant Bridge, which was inadequate in handling the increased traffic of daily life, as well as to overcome the design flaws of the earlier bridge, in which insufficient height clearance prevented river boats from passing safely under it during high tide.

Read Bridge was officially opened by Governor Cecil Clementi Smith on 18 April 1889. River traffic was able to operate in all tide conditions and this greatly facilitated commerce.

The area surrounding Read Bridge was a predominant Teochew district. Its residents were mainly coolies, boatmen and lightermen by profession, and worked to support the river trade. For many years right up to the 1960s, Read Bridge was a popular night entertainment venue by the river. One could find storytellers relating stories to labourers, as well as small-scale street operas being performed.

CLIFFORD PIER

Named after Sir Hugh Clifford, Governor of the Straits Settlements in 1933, Clifford Pier was constructed as a landing point for travellers arriving by sea into Singapore. It replaced Johnston's Pier that had been in operation for over 75 years since 1855.

For many years, Clifford Pier was known as Red Lamp Pier in vernacular Chinese. This was in reference to a red oil lamp hung from the pier that served as a guide to seamen.

The pier was designed in 1930 by Frank Dorrington Ward, Chief Architect of the Public Works Department. The building's Art Deco entrance is topped by a sculptured emblem of the Straits Settlements of Singapore. Stepping into the building, one will be greeted by a large hall with a roof consisting of concrete arched trusses.

Clifford Pier had been the venue for day travellers taking boat rides to the Southern Islands for several years. On 1 April 2006 however, the pier was closed when the sea traffic was relocated to Marina South Pier. This was in line with the government's efforts to convert Marina Bay into a fresh water reservoir as an integral part of the greater Marina Barrage project.

The Urban Redevelopment Authority gazetted Clifford Pier and its adjacent former Customs Harbor branch building as conservation buildings. The national planning authority had zoned these for development into an integrated retail, leisure and entertainment centre. These would complement the waterfront development of Marina Bay.

Clifford Pier has started a new chapter of life as a restaurant. As part of Sino Group's Fullerton Heritage project to develop the historical waterfront, the building has undergone restoration and adaptive re-use to house an international restaurant and bar with alfresco dinning.

Clifford Pier
70 Collyer Quay
S(049323)

FAMILY AND JUVENILE COURT

This site played a very important role in the import and supply of Chinese immigrant labour to Singapore and British Malaya during the 19th and early 20th centuries. The current building that we see today was the second building of the Chinese Protectorate, designed by H. Stallwood in 1928.

The Chinese Protectorate was established in 1833. William Pickering was appointed as the first Chinese Protector, and was responsible for protecting and controlling Chinese immigrants in Singapore. Staffed by British officers conversant in Chinese language and dialects, the Chinese Protectorate controlled the Chinese coolie traffic. As the main contact point between the colonial government and the Chinese community, these officials oversaw a wide range

of functions and duties, which included mediating Chinese labour disputes, monitoring activities of Chinese triads and secret societies, as well as curbing gambling and vices. In the early 20th century, the Chinese Protectorate's functions were expanded to monitor and control the political activities of the Overseas Chinese participation in the Singapore branches of the Nationalist Party of China (Kuomintang).

In post-war Singapore, the Chinese Protectorate was abolished by the colonial government, and its functions were assumed by new administrative outfits set up within the colony of Singapore. These included the departments of education, immigration, labour and social welfare.

Family and
Juvenile Court

3 Havelock Square
S(059725)

Following internal self-government in 1955, the Ministry of Labour and Social Welfare was based in this building. In 1959, this became the Ministry of Labour and Law, which also occupied this building. The Ministry of Labour remained here until 1990.

Restored in early 2000, this building is now used as the Family and Juvenile Court. It is a gazetted National Monument of Singapore.

JAMAE MOSQUE

If you are in Chinatown, do look out for the Jamae Mosque located at the junction of Mosque Street and South Bridge Road. This mosque tells an interesting story of Singapore's early history.

The founding of modern Singapore by the British East India Company in 1819 saw the convergence of people and resources from all parts of the world on this little island at the southern point of the Malay Peninsula. Amongst one of the earliest immigrant groups that came to Singapore were the Chulias, who contributed much to the economic success of this island. The Chulias were South Indian Muslims from the Coromandel Coast. They were traders and money changers who had been trading in the Malayo-Indonesian region (present-day Malaysia, Singapore and Indonesia) since the days of the Dutch East India Company. With the founding of the new port by the British, they expanded their operations to Singapore, and eventually settled down here.

This early Chulia community resided near the Singapore River, and that area became known as Chulia Street. This street is now occupied by high-rise office buildings in Raffles Place.

Within a few years of Singapore's founding, a member of the Chulia community by the name of Ansar Saib erected a mosque at South Bridge Road between 1826 and 1827. This early mosque was later replaced by the Jamae Mosque, which was built between 1830 and 1835. The Chulias also built the Masjid Al-Abrar on Telok Ayer Street, as well as the Nagore Durgha. Both are located in the Chinatown district and are now part of the Chinatown Conservation Area.

The Jamae Mosque features Indian architecture that is similar to the Nagore Durgha shrine. A pair of towers flanks its main entrance.

Jamae Mosque
218 South Bridge Road
S(058767)

These identical towers have pairs of small niches between delicate, horizontal mouldings, and a miniature dome on top. However, the foyer, main prayer hall, ancillary prayer hall and shrine all evoke Singapore architecture of the 1830s; the influence of architect G.D. Coleman is seen in the Neo-Classical design of this section.

While there were plans to renovate and rebuild the mosque in 1897 and 1911, such efforts were not successful, and the mosque continued to retain its original structure.

The Jamae Mosque was gazetted as a National Monument on 29 November 1974. It underwent repairs and repainting in 1996, and is now owned by the Majlis Ugama Islam Singapura (MUIS).

JINRIKISHA STATION

Standing prominently at the junction of Neil Road and Tanjong Pagar Road is a two-storey building with a dome-shaped roof, first constructed between 1903 and 1904 to be the main *jinrikisha* (rickshaw) depot.

For five decades between the 1880s and 1930s, the *jinrikisha*, also known as *kreta Hong Kong* in colloquial Malay, was the dominant mode of short-distance public transport in Singapore. The Jinrikisha Station was a public building administered by the Jinrikisha Department, which was responsible for registering, licensing and controlling the *jinrikisha* industry. Municipal Engineer Samuel Tomlinson and Municipal Architect D.M. Craik were responsible for the design of this building.

The Jinrikisha Station is now a part of the Tanjong Pagar Conservation Area. In December 2007, Hong Kong movie star Jackie Chan became the owner of the Jinrikisha Station building, having purchased it from a Singapore property group at a price of $11 million.

Jinrikisha Station
1 Neil Road S(088804)

THE JINRIKISHA

Invented by the Japanese in 1869, the *jinrikisha*—a compact, lightweight two-wheeled cart—was designed to be a carriage pulled by one or more men. As a cheap and convenient form of transportation for the masses, the *jinrikisha* was introduced to China, India and Southeast Asia. In 1883, there were some 2,000 *jinrikishas* in Singapore. At the turn of the 20th century though, more than 20,000 licensed *jinrikishas* were plying the roads of the municipality. Chinese *jinrikisha* pullers were a familiar sight on Singapore's streets, providing transportation for the common people commuting within the vicinity of Tanjong Pagar, North and South Bridge Roads, Raffles Place and Beach Road. Fares were calculated at a rate of three cents for half a mile in 1904.

By the 1930s, *jinrikishas* were gradually being phased out by the trishaw as the common transport mode of the day. Many *jinrikisha* pullers moved on to become trishaw operators as the use of the bicycle to power a carriage was superior to that of a puller. After World War II, the *jinrikisha* was confined to the history books, having been fully replaced by the trishaw.

LAU PA SAT (Telok Ayer Market)

Nestled within the tall, glass-cladded skyscrapers along Shenton Way and Robinson Road is a cast iron Victorian-era building, which features an octagonal-shaped roof capped with a four-faced clock tower. A familiar landmark since 1894, this is the Telok Ayer Market.

Constructed in 1894 by the Singapore Municipality, the Telok Ayer Market replaced an earlier fish market that was used for seven decades since 1825. This market used to be sited along the sea shore, where jetties allowed the easy loading and unloading of produce and seafood from boats to the market. However, with the commencement of the Telok Ayer reclamation project in the 1870s, the market was demolished as it caused obstruction to reclamation works.

In 1894, Telok Ayer Market was revived with the construction of a new cast iron building on the newly-reclaimed land. It was designed by Municipal Engineer James MacRitchie (after whom MacRitchie Reservoir is named). To retain the memory of the previous market designed by G.D. Coleman, MacRitchie matched its octagonal shape for the new market.

MacRitchie was inspired by the Crystal Palace exhibition hall in London's Hyde Park, an architectural design masterpiece of the mid-19th century by Joseph Paxton. Paxton had demonstrated that it was possible to design and construct a modern building utilising parts that were factory-built and pre-fabricated for on-site assembly. Adopting the latest revolutionary building technology of the 19th century, MacRitchie's new market was constructed using cast iron parts prefabricated in Glasgow, Scotland by P&W MacLallan. These parts were shipped to Singapore, and the building was assembled on site by Riley Hargreaves & Co.

Lau Pa Sat

18 Raffles Quay
S(048582)

With cast iron being the dominant building material, MacRitchie paid attention to craftsmanship and detail in ensuring that the cast iron objects further served as a decorative element. The building was held up by cast iron archways, fretted eaves brackets and columns that feature composite capitals supporting trusses with filigree-like infills.

In 1897, the Municipal Government constructed a new market at the bank of the Singapore River along Ellenborough Street. Overnight, Ellenborough Market became known to local residents as the new market (*Pasar Baru*), and Telok Ayer Market was henceforth labelled as the old market (*Lau Pasar*). Ellenbourough Market remained in use until it was engulfed in a fire in 1968, and demolished the following year.

Telok Ayer Market ceased to be a wet market after it was successfully converted into a hawker food centre in 1973. It remained a food centre until 1986, when it was temporarily closed to facilitate the construction of the Mass Rapid Transit system. The cast iron parts were systematically disassembled and catalogued to facilitate its future re-assembly.

Since 1991, the restored Telok Ayer Market has re-opened as a 24-hour hawker food centre with a new brand name—Lau Pa Sat Festival Market. It is a gazetted National Monument of Singapore.

NAGORE DARGAH

The Nagore Dargah was constructed between 1828 and 1830 by the Singapore Indian-Muslim community to commemorate a 15th-century holy man named Shabul Hamid Durgha of Nagore, South India.

This 180-year-old building ranks amongst one of the longest-standing structures in Singapore. Dating from the early days of the British East India-administered settlement of Singapore, this Islamic shrine is the oldest building in Telok Ayer, and also the oldest Muslim and Indian structure on the island.

The building's architectural features are both rare and unique within Singapore. This square structure's façade comprises four corners linked by an elaborate balustrade that screens the roof from

the street. Each corner has a 14-level square minaret that is topped by an onion-shaped dome and a finial at the apex.

Gazetted as a National Monument in 1974, the Nagore Dargah is administered by the trustees of the Jamae Mosque and owned by Majlis Ugama Islam Singapura (MUIS).

This building has been restored at a cost of $2 million for its new use as an Indian-Muslim Heritage Centre.

OLD THONG CHAI MEDICAL INSTITUTION

Amongst the shopping malls at Eu Tong Sen Street stands a small Chinese Cantonese-style building with s green tiled roof and big Chinese lanterns hung outside its wooden doors. If you guess that it is a legacy from Singapore's yesteryears, you are correct. This is the Old Thong Chai Building.

To many older Singaporeans, this building is better known as the Thong Chai Medical Institution. It was one of the first Chinese

medical institutions available to Chinese immigrants in Singapore during the late 19th century.

Singapore's founding as a free port in 1819 provided tremendous opportunities for Chinese immigrants seeking employment and a chance at securing better standards of living. The subsequent massive influx of people to Singapore witnessed the creation of many clan and social associations catering to their needs. Medical services were one of those in demand, with many Chinese immigrants relying on traditional Chinese medical treatment instead of unfamiliar Western medication.

Singapore's early Chinese medical institutions were established by wealthy Chinese philanthropic merchants and clan associations. These were the Chinese Pauper Hospital (built in 1884), Fei Choon Free Hospital (1890), Thong Chai Medical Institution (1892), Kiung Chow Loke Tin Kee Hospital (1902) and Kwong Wai Siu Free Hospital (1910).

The Thong Chai Yee Say was established in 1837 to provide free medical consultation and medication for all people irrespective of race, religion and status. In 1892, the institution moved into a new building at Wayang Street (now called Eu Tong Sen Street) as the result of fund-raising efforts by Mr Gan Eng Seng, a philanthropist and founder of Gan Eng Seng School. The British Colonial Government had also helped by providing the land for the building. Thong Chai Yee Say was renamed Thong Chai Medical Institution following this move.

Besides being a medical institution, the building served as a meeting point for various Chinese interests, such as being the headquarters for Singapore's Chinese guild. It was also the first headquarters of the Singapore Chinese Chamber of Commerce.

Old Thong Chai
Medical Institution

50 Eu Tong Sen Street
S(059803)

同濟醫院

On 6 July 1973, Thong Chai Medical Institution made history by becoming the first building to be gazetted as a National Monument of Singapore. In 1975, it moved to its new 10-storey premises at Chin Swee Road. The existing building has since undergone different uses such as an arts and crafts centre, a discotheque and a fusion restaurant known as ASIAN.

Thong Chai Medical Institution has faithfully provided medical consultation to the community for over 130 years. Today, it has six specialist departments in the areas of acupuncture, gerontology, cancer, infertility, nephropathy and orthopaedic massotherapy.

Architectural Features

The Old Thong Chai Medical Institution building is very unique within modern Singapore, and is a rare surviving example of Southern Chinese secular architecture. Notable features of this structure include its ornate carvings, huge pillars and beams. There is a front and a back entrance facing Eu Tong Sen Street and New Market Road respectively. At the main entrance is a granite stela inscribed with four Chinese characters.

The building's four halls are arranged along a central axis, separated by two courtyards and an airwell. Two of these halls are double-storey structures constructed in the Southern Chinese palace style. A pair of wooden staircases leads to the upper floors.

SRI MARIAMMAN TEMPLE

Sri Mariamman Temple takes its place as the oldest Hindu temple in Singapore. This temple is located in the heart of Chinatown, and the local road, Temple Street, was so named in its honour. It was first constructed in 1827 by Naraina Pillay, an Indian pioneer who came to Singapore's shores with Sir Stamford Raffles in 1819. He was a government clerk from Penang who settled down in Singapore.

The earliest wood and attap structure was subsequently replaced with a brick building in 1844. Since then, this building has undergone several alterations and additions periodically.

Sri Mariamman Temple played an important role in the lives of Singapore Hindus. In the early days, it helped new immigrants to settle down in Singapore. It also served as the Registry of Marriages for Hindus when the temple's priests were authorised to solemnise Hindu marriages.

The dominant feature of the temple's South Indian architectural heritage is the *gopuram* (entrance tower). The *gopuram* was first

Sri Mariamman Temple

244 South Bridge Road S(058793)

built in 1903, and the present six-tiered tower was added in 1925. Its height signals its presence to the devotees from afar, so that they can prepare for their prayer or meditation at the temple.

On the *gopuram* are displays of Hindu deities and their reincarnations in various poses. These are flanked by a statue of Murugan (the Lord of War) and the blue Krishna. Among the various Hindu deities, one can also notice Indian Sepoy soldiers located within the *gopuram*.

The temple's parapets are adorned with sculptures of sacred cows. The bull is honoured as Nandi, the mount of Siva. Its presence indicates that the temple is a Saivite temple. On the western elevation are four *vimanam* (domes) that signify the presence of a shrine or altar beneath them for the Hindu deities.

Sri Mariamman Temple was gazetted as a National Monument on 6 July 1973. The temple is currently preparing for its next restoration process and a consecration ceremony is scheduled to take place in April 2010.

TELOK AYER CHINESE METHODIST CHURCH

Founded in 1889 by Dr Benjamin West at a shophouse in Boon Tat Street, Telok Ayer Chinese Methodist Church is one of the oldest Chinese Methodist churches in Singapore. During its early years, the church functioned out of shophouses within the Telok Ayer district.

In 1921, the church purchased some land at this site (belonging to the Chinese Free School, now known as Gan Eng Seng School), and began a fund-raising campaign for a permanent church building. This building was constructed in 1924 at a cost of $46,000 for use by a Hokkien-speaking congregation. The foundation stone was laid on 19 January 1924 by Bishop G.H. Bickley, and consecrated the following year on 11 January 1925 by Bishop Titus Lowe.

Architectural Features

Designed by the architectural firm Swan & MacLaren, the church's design reflects a mix of western and Chinese elements. Constructed with bricks and concrete, this rectangular, three-storey structure with a Chinese rooftop pavilion is a modern 20th-century building that reflects the Chinese character of its occupants. At the street level on the west side, the building has a five-foot way comprising a row of columns marked with crosses, giving it a Christian identity. In some ways, the church features a Chinese "National Style" architectural typology that appeared in Republican China.

Gazetted as a National Monument in 1989, Telok Ayer Chinese Methodist Church embarked on a two-year restoration project in 1993 at a cost of $3 million.

Telok Ayer Chinese Methodist Church

235 Telok Ayer Street S(068656)

THIAN HOCK KENG TEMPLE

The Thian Hock Keng is one of Singapore's most majestic Chinese temples. It was built during the days when Telok Ayer Street was still a sandy beach crowded with small sailing craft—long before the first land reclamation began the inexorable separation of the temple from the seashore, which was the very reason for its existence.

Prior to the temple's construction, a shrine or "joss house" to *Ma Zu Po* or *Tian Hou* (Mother of Heavenly Sages) was erected on the site soon after the first Chinese immigrants followed Stamford Raffles ashore. It was here where new arrivals from China's Fujian province showed their gratitude to the goddess for a voyage safely ended. As such, the history of the Thian Hock Keng is firmly associated with the Fujian community.

Efforts to build the temple were led by Malacca-born pioneer and philantropist Tan Tock Seng (1798–1850), who was the largest contributor of funds. This and other details of the temple's history are recorded in granite tablets on the wall immediately inside the entrance hall. There is also a timber calligraphy panel presented by Qing Dynasty Emperor Guang Xu in 1907, lending evidence to the temple's stature.

With the ravages of two world wars and subsequent decades of urban reclamation and redevelopment, the temple began to crumble. Its tiled courtyard—cracked and overrun by muck, sweat, tears and offerings of visiting worshippers—began to disintegrate. Its airy ceilings, which soaked up a century-and-a-half's worth of warm ash, developed a musty grey lacquer. The temple's owners,

Singapore Hokkien Huay Kuan, closed it for its third major renovation in 1998.

The traditional method for Chinese temple restoration involved a top-down approach, commencing from the roof and proceeding downwards to the foundations. Seventy craftsmen, together with a Beijing University-trained contractor, were brought in to dismantle and reassemble the temple's parts. Roof tiles, timber boards, columns and beams were systemically removed. Undamaged items were salvaged and retained for re-use while damaged items were repaired and replaced by skilled craftsmen. The spirals and dancing dragon motifs adorning the roof ridges and hips were repaired with the use of traditional *jian nian* and lacquer paste. In accordance with the traditional post-and-beam style of timber joinery, not a single nail was used to secure the arches.

Three years, $3.5 million and 30,000 roof tiles later, the temple's beauty and splendour was restored. The building now stands with magnificent stature among giant office skyscrapers, and its doors open to welcome the public.

The restored Thian Hock Keng Temple was recognised by the United Nations with the UNESCO Asia-Pacific Heritage Conservation Award (Honourable Mention) in 2001. This was the first Singapore building to ever receive UNESCO affirmation.

Thian Hock Keng Temple
158 Telok Ayer Street
S(068613)

Architectural Features

The temple is built in traditional Southern Chinese architectural style. There are three distinct parts to the complex, each with its own entrance. In the centre is the temple itself. To the right is a long, narrow plot containing the premises of the Keng Teck Huat, or Family Benefit Society; and to the left is a square compound with the Chung Wen Pagoda and Chong Hock Pavilion.

The temple design adheres to the Chinese principle of axial symmetry. Positioned along a central north-to-south axis, the three halls—entrance, main (housing the main altar to Ma Zu) and rear (housing an altar to Guanyin, the Goddess of Mercy)—are built on raised podiums to underscore their importance. They are separated by open-air courtyards lined with single-storey buildings. The exposed beams and cantilevered brackets are richly carved with heroes at war, sages on horseback, saints on clouds and patterns of flowers and animals, all enhanced by red-and-black lacquer guilded in gold.

The temple's roofscape is its crowning glory. It consists of curved ridges, elongated eaves with upturned Minnan (Southern Fujian) "swallow tail" end sweeps and generous ornamentation. Surmounting the entrance hall's roof are a blazing pearl and four dancing dragons. These dragons symbolise strength, justice and authority, and they are shown striving towards the perfection of ideas and concepts as represented by the pearl.

It is interesting to note that in such traditional temple architecture, there are several eclectic European decorative touches, from the glazed ceramic tiles forming the dado on the exterior wall to the cast iron railings along the front of the temple.

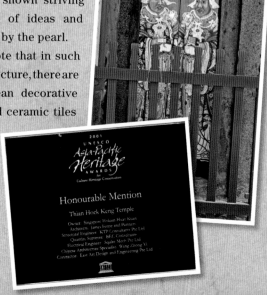

JIAN NIAN

Jian Nian is a traditional ornamental decoration involving porcelain mosaic work. Using coloured rice bowls, the craftsmen clip the porcelain into various shaped shards and proceed to fix them onto lime plaster bas reliefs to form vibrant colourful representations of traditional religious mythology and symbols. This is a cultural craft of the Fujian and Teochew people.

YUE HWA DEPARTMENT STORE
(FORMER SOUTHERN HOTEL)

When first constructed in 1927, the Southern Hotel was the tallest landmark in Chinatown. It was also one of the most modern buildings of its time, being the first Chinese hotel to feature a lift. This six-storey building housed offices on the ground floor, while hotel rooms occupied the upper floors. A Chinese restaurant and tea house operated at the roof terrace, where occasional Chinese opera performances were held.

Designed by the architectural firm Swan & MacLaren, this building exhibits the Modern Movement style that symbolises an era of speed, light and revolutionary production. With functionality in mind, the façade has only the bare essentials. These include the

Yue Hwa
Department Store

70 Eu Tong Sen Street
S(059805)

industrial-like designs of the metal framed windows and the angular arches of the first-storey arcade, which only serve to reinforce this architectural style.

The building ceased to be a hotel in the 1980s. Under the management of the Yue Hwa Department Store, it has been restored, and also undergone a process of adaptive re-use for its new lease of life as an emporium selling Chinese products.

This historical landmark of Singapore's Chinatown is a gazetted conservation building.

YUEH HAI CHING TEMPLE

Situated in the Central Business District and within walking distance from the banks of the Singapore River is a small Chinese temple that has served the Chinese Teochew community for over 180 years, making it Singapore's oldest Teochew temple.

The Yueh Hai Ching Temple (literally translated as 'Guangdong Calm Sea Temple'), also known as *Wang Hai Cheng Bio* in vernacular Teochew, was first constructed on this site in 1826 as a wood and attap shrine. It was built to allow merchants, sailors, fishermen and other travellers to express their gratitude towards the Chinese deities for blessing them with a safe sea journey from China to Singapore. The worshippers would extend their thanks to the patron deities of Heavenly Father (*Xuan Tian Shang Di*) and Heavenly Mother (*Tien Hou*) installed in the temple.

Over the ensuing decades, the temple was expanded through new construction and renovations. In the 19th century, two phases of work took place from 1852 to 1855, and from 1859 to 1896. This resulted in the temple assuming the architectural form that we now see.

On religious festive occasions, traditional Chinese operas are staged on temporary platforms erected within the open courtyard space. Worshippers and the public would attend the performances held on the temple grounds.

Owned by the Ngee Ann Kongsi (a prominent Teochew clan association founded in 1845), Yueh Hai Ching Temple was gazetted as a National Monument in 1996.

Architectural Features

Possessing a mix of Chaozhou and Zhangzhou architectural styles, this temple is located within a large, enclosed courtyard. Stepping through the main doorway, one has to walk further into the courtyard in order to reach the main building. Constructed on an east-to-west axis, the courtyard and building forms a private Southern Chinese cultural world for those within the confines of the temple grounds.

The roofscape of the temple forms a unique feature of the built structure. The elaborate and intricate porcelain shard (known as *jian nian*) seen here is a characteristic of Chaozhou architecture. This craft handiwork involved the use of clay sculptures to decorate the roof. These individual sculptures were cemented with colourful cut porcelain shards to form an intended relief image of flora, fauna, human and mythical birds. Collectively, they contribute to the aesthetics of the building's architecture.

The respective shrines of Xuan Tian Shang Di and Tien Hou are differentiated by the roof ridges to their entrances. A roof ridge exhibiting two dragons chasing a flaming pearl marks the entrance to the shrine of Xuan Tian Shang Di, while the other roof displaying two dragons guarding a pagoda indicates the shrine of Tien Hou. The two shrines are linked within the temple building through an internal doorway layout.

The front of the entrance hall has panels displaying elaborate relief plaster figurines in traditional scenes from Chinese opera.

These handiworks are good examples of traditional Southern Chinese craftwork.

Within the temple, visitors can view the exposed structural elements of this traditional building. The interior displays a Zhangzhou style of the structural framing system. Supporting the roof truss system are Zhangzhou-style pumpkin struts and hanging struts.

Yueh Hai Ching Temple

30B Phillip Street
S(048696)

EAST BANK

ARMENIAN CHURCH OF SINGAPORE

Dating from the immediate years of Singapore's founding, the Armenian Church of St Gregory is the oldest Christian church building in Singapore. In 1824, there was a community of 16 Armenians residing in Singapore. The early Armenian immigrants felt the need to establish a church for their community, and in tandem with fund-raising efforts that commenced in 1827, the community received a plot of land at Hill Street to build the church in 1833.

The church was constructed in 1835 and consecrated as the Church of St Gregory the Illuminator. Built at a cost of 5,000 Spanish dollars, half of the funds were contributed by the 16 Singapore Armenians, while another 25 per cent came from Armenians residing in British India and Dutch Java. The balance was raised from well-wishers in the Singapore European and Chinese mercantile communities.

During the early years, the church was the centre of the small Armenian community's activities; social gatherings, weddings, baptisms and funerals took place there. Succeeding generations of Armenians took upon the responsibilities of keeping the church in good shape. Through all these, the church has helped the Armenian community retain their cultural and national identity.

The church had a resident priest for many years. However, with the Armenian population dwindling due to migration and death, Orthodox Armenian services are no longer held on a regular basis at the church.

The Armenian Church of Singapore was gazetted as a National Monument on 6 July 1973.

Architectural Features

With a maximum seating capacity of 55, this small, white building was designed by architect G.D. Coleman, Overseer of Convicts and Superintendent of Public Works. He built the church in the 19th-century Neo-Classical Palladin style—the style that Coleman is believed to have introduced to Singapore.

The church design has been likened to a piece of handsomely set jewel, with porticos on three sides of small but stately proportions. It was modelled after St Gregory's Church in Echmiadzin (the mother church in Northern Armenia), but modified to suit local tropical conditions.

On the north, south and west fronts of the church are Tuscan Doric porticos capped with triangular pediments. These porticos were designed to allow horse carriages to move into the porches, right up to the doors of the church. The porches were on the same level as the base of horse carriages so as to facilitate easy movement from the carriage to the church without having to step on the ground.

The east front, where the main entrance is, bears an elegant bowed apse with a pediment into which "1835" is carved to commemorate the year the church's foundation was laid.

The interior of the church is circular in shape. This concept was thought to have been derived from the circular design of St Martin-in-the Fields, an Anglican Church located at Trafalgar Square,

London. Others have thought the inspiration came from the Round Church (officially known as Holy Sepulchre Church) at Cambridge. Regardless, Coleman added his personal touch by enclosing the circle within a rectangular structure.

There was originally a domed roof and a bell-turret on the building. In 1853, these were found to be structurally unsafe, and were demolished. In their place now is a square tower.

A parsonage was added to the grounds in 1905. The parsonage—a two-storey bungalow that served as the residence of the priest—was built by Mrs Nanajan Sarkies in memory of her late husband, John Shanazar Sarkies. Also present in the grounds is a memorial garden, which has a number of tombstones of early Armenian residents. These tombstones were transported from the Christian cemetery in Bukit Timah after their graves were exhumed in 1988.

Armenian Church of Singapore

60 Hill Street
S(179366)

ARTS HOUSE AT THE OLD PARLIAMENT

The Old Parliament House is one of the oldest buildings in Singapore. Since its construction in 1826 by G.D. Coleman as a residence for John Argyle Maxwell, a Scottish merchant, the house has been a key witness to Singapore's history for over 180 years.

Permission for its construction had in fact been issued in error, as this area was not zoned for residential use under the Raffles Town Plan of 1822. Rather, it was zoned for government use. In 1827, the house was rented by the government for use as Singapore's first Court House. However, a decision was taken to construct a new court house along High Street, where the courts moved and remained until 1875 when a decision was made to relocate back to the previous house. The Court House then became the Supreme Court of Singapore until 1939.

Following the move of the court house, the 19th century Neo-Classical building became known as the Secretariat to house the public administrative offices of the municipal government. In the following years, it also served as the offices of the Government Printer and the Attorney-General Chambers.

During the early 20th century, the Court House was further renovated and space was added to extend the building. Amongst the significant changes was the alteration of the external façade from English Palladianism to late Victorian.

In post-war Singapore, the house was identified for new usage as a Legislative Assembly building. After renovations and conversion work took place between 1953 and 1954 with the installation of a legislative chamber, the Singapore Legislative Assembly House was officially opened by Governor Sir John Nicoll on 7 July 1954. Singapore attained internal self-government the following year, and full sovereign independence 10 years later.

The Legislative Assembly House then became the Parliament of Singapore in 1965.

Arts House at The Old Parliament

1 Old Parliament Lane
S(179429)

Singapore's legislature functioned out of this building for 45 years until Parliament moved to its new building at 1 Parliament Place in October 1999. The building underwent a $15-million restoration to become a venue for performance and the visual arts known as the Arts House. The former parliamentary chamber was preserved, while other sections of the building were converted for new usage. These included a Thai restaurant occupying the annex, and the addition of a 75-seat theatre at the ground floor.

Siamese Elephant Statue

Along the side of the Old Parliament House is the Siamese Elephant Statue, facing the direction of the Padang. This structure commemorates the visit of Siamese King Chulalongkorn in 1871, and about 140 years of friendship between Singapore and Thailand.

The Kingdom of Siam (now known as Thailand) had a new King ascending the throne upon the death of King Mongkut (Rama IV) in 1868. He was a 15-year-old boy named Somdetch Phra Paramindr Maha Chulalongkorn (Rama V), better known as King Chulalongkorn.

As monarch for 40 years, King Chulalongkorn was well-respected for modernising his country and expanding ties with other countries, Singapore being the first foreign land he visited in his life. It was a historical event, as it was the first foreign trip ever to be undertaken by a Siamese monarch.

On 16 March 1871, the King and his entourage landed at Johnston's Pier and were received by the officer administering the government, Colonel A.E.H. Anson. He was a guest at Government House (now known as the Istana) and visited many local places. A week later, the King left for the next leg of his foreign tour to Batavia (now known as Jakarta).

After returning to Siam, the King decided to present a gift of a bronze elephant to Singapore as a token of his thanks as well as a commemoration of his visit. The Elephant Statue was unveiled in front of the Town Hall (now known as Victoria Memorial Hall) on 25 June 1872. For the next 47 years, the Elephant Statue was sited on that spot.

As part of Singapore's centenary celebrations in 1919, the colonial government relocated both the Elephant Statue and the Sir Stamford Raffles statue to new sites. The Raffles statue was placed in front of the Victoria Memorial Hall, while the Elephant Statue was repositioned next to the Court House (Old Parliament House). The Elephant Statue is a gazetted National Monument of Singapore.

CATHEDRAL OF GOOD SHEPHERD

Singapore's first Roman Catholic church building was constructed at Bras Basah Road on the site of the former St Joseph's Institution in 1833. Made out of wood and attap, this early church building could not cope with the growing needs of the local Catholic community, and plans were made for the construction of a larger church elsewhere.

A site at Queen Street was thus selected, and a fund-raising drive commenced in 1840. The cornerstone was laid on 18 June 1843 by John Connolly, having been blessed by Bishop J.P. Courvezy. Upon its completion and at a cost of $18,355, the church was consecrated by Father Beurel on 6 June 1846. This building has served the Catholic community ever since.

Over the years, the building underwent various additions. In 1847 the steeple, designed by Charles Alexander Dyce, was erected. Marble paving was installed in 1860, while the nave was extended by three bays to its present length in 1888. A pipe organ was added to the church in 1912.

The church was elevated to the status of cathedral in 1888 with the revival of the Diocese of Malacca, but its consecration ceremony by Bishop Rene Fee only took place on 14 February 1897.

Within the compound are two 19th-century bungalows, which are among the oldest buildings in this district. These are the Archbishop's House and the Priest's Residence. At the corner of the compound facing Victoria Street is the two-storey Archbishop's House. This 1859 bungalow features green porcelain bottle-shaped balusters on the first-level balustrade. The two-storey Priest's Residence, constructed in 1911, features a rusticated base and decorative plasterwork.

The Cathedral of the Good Shepherd is a gazetted National Monument of Singapore.

CENTRAL FIRE STATION

Built in 1909 by the Singapore Municipality, the Central Fire Station was Singapore's first proper fire station. It came about from the re-organisation of the Singapore Fire Brigade in 1905 under the command of Fire Brigade Superintendent Montague Pett, who also oversaw the construction of the station.

The completed building had a dozen bays for fire engines and rescue vehicles to be dispatched during emergency, as well as a watch tower and living quarters for firemen. The three-storey structure was first designed for use by horse-drawn fire engines, but it successfully made the transition to house motorised vehicles in 1912.

This fire station had been in continuous service for a century. As Singapore oldest fire station, it witnessed the growth of the Fire Brigade and the professionalism of the Singapore Fire Service when it became the Singapore Civil Defence Force.

Featuring a Neo-Classical architectural style, the red-and-white brick building is one of two buildings from the Edwardian period that remains in Singapore.

Gazetted as a National Monument of Singapore, a section of Central Fire Station was adapted for new usage as the Civil Defence Heritage Gallery. This gallery showcases the history of the Fire Service through exhibits of fire engines, fire-fighting equipment and uniforms of yesteryear; and tracks its development and contributions to civil defence since the 19th century. The staff quarters within the rear of the compound were redeveloped and upgraded with new quarters and bays to cater to larger modern fire engines, while the Chief Fire Officer's house has been converted into a restaurant.

Central Fire
Station

62 Hill Street
S(179367)

CHIJMES

Located along Victoria Street is CHIJMES, a popular local lifestyle and recreational complex. Yet this cluster of historical buildings comprising Caldwell House, the Chapel and other structures had been a Catholic convent and orphanage during the first phase of its existence.

In the mid-19th century, Father Jean Marie Beurel saw the need for an orphanage for abandoned children and a Catholic school for local girls. Caldwell House was acquired in 1852 to be the residences of French nuns of the order of the Holy Infant Jesus. For many years, abandoned babies and young children would be left at the "small gate" for the care of the Catholic nuns. A signboard now commemorates this small gate—the Gate of Good Hope—located at the corner of Bras Basah Road and Victoria Street. Constructed in the 1840s by G.D. Coleman, Caldwell House ranks amongst one of the oldest buildings in Singapore.

Land in the surrounding plot was acquired and added to the estate of the Convent of the Holy Infant Jesus (CHIJ) in 1854. The Chapel was constructed at the turn of the 20th century, and was consecrated in 1904. Father Charles Benedict Nain was responsible for its Neo-Gothic design, believed to be inspired by French church architecture. This chapel features colourful stained glass windows and column capitals.

After 129 years as a Catholic girls school and convent, CHIJ closed its doors in 1983. These buildings were gazetted for preservation by the Preservation of Monuments Board in 1990, and an extensive restoration programme was planned and implemented for Caldwell House and the Chapel.

The restoration work sought to retain the buildings' original structural and architectural elements. In restoring the Chapel's stained glass windows, the broken glass pieces were repaired by French specialists in line with original materials as well as authentic skills and craftsmanship. Italian experts were recruited to oversee the cleaning and restoration of the buildings façades and column capitals. This arduous work took over a decade before reaching full completion.

CHIJ opened its doors to the public as CHIJMES in the late 1990s. Its completed restoration work received the endorsement of UNESCO with the UNESCO Asia Pacific Heritage Awards for Culture Heritage Conservation Merit Award in 2002.

2002
UNESCO
Asia-Pacific
Heritage
AWARDS
for
Culture Heritage Conservation

Award of Merit
Convent of the Holy Infant Jesus

Owner: CHIJMES Investment Pte Ltd

Architect: Ong & Ong Architects Pte Ltd
General Contractor: Low Keng Huat (S) Ltd

Chijmes
30 Victoria Street
S(187996)

CHURCH OF OUR LADY OF LOURDES

The Church of Our Lady of Lourdes is Singapore's first Indian Catholic church. Prior to the church's construction in 1888, Indian Catholics had worshipped at the Cathedral of the Good Shepherd as well as at the Church of Sts Peter and Paul.

The Catholic Church received a grant for the land site at Ophir Road from the Straits Settlements Government in 1885, and a decision was made to build the Church of Our Lady of Lourdes. Designed by Mr A.W. Lermitt of the architectural firm Swan & MacLaren, this church was designed in the Neo-Gothic style, and inspired by the Basilica at Lourdes, France.

No expenses were spared in the construction of the church. Directly imported from France were the pointed arches, spires, flying buttresses and 16 slender pillars. The stained glass windows of the church illustrate the 15 mysteries of the Most Holy Rosary. This is the only historical building in Singapore with stained glass windows depicting the story of the original Church of Lourdes in France. Just next to the main entrance are cast iron spiral staircases that lead up to an upper gallery. Within the church interior, one can see Corinthian columns with gold-leafed capitals.

The compound also had a vicarage and a Tamil school for the children of the parishioners.

While this church was originally designated for the primary use of Indian Catholics, the Catholic Church declared this church to be 'territorial' in 1974, and opened its doors to all people regardless of their ethnicity.

In January 2005, the Preservation of Monuments Board gazetted this church as a National Monument of Singapore.

CHURCH OF STS PETER AND PAUL

Located next to the Singapore Art Museum (former St Joseph's Institution) is the Church of Sts Peter and Paul, built between 1869 and 1870 by Father Pierre Paris, who headed the Chinese Catholic Mission. This is Singapore's oldest Chinese Catholic church, and it

Church of Our
Lady of Lourdes

50 Ophir Road
S(188690)

is responsible for the later founding of the Church of the Sacred Heart, Church of Our Lady of Lourdes, Church of the Nativity of the Blessed Virgin Mary, St Teresa's Church and other parishes.

The Church of Sts Peter and Paul was erected to provide a place of worship for the increasing number of Chinese converts in Singapore. According to Song Ong Siang in *One Hundred Years' History of the Chinese* in Singapore, Pedro Tan No Keah, an influential man among the Chinese Catholics during the 1860s, subscribed liberally toward the cost of building the church. Interestingly, Walter Makepeace pointed out in *One Hundred Years of Singapore* that Emperor Napoleon III of France had defrayed the cost of the church's compound wall.

Since the establishment of the church, the priests of this parish had always been appointed the head of the Chinese Catholic Mission in Singapore. Consequently, the Church of Sts Peter and Paul became the "Seat" of the Chinese (Asiatic) Catholics of Singapore. Most notably, many Singapore Catholic parishes trace their roots to this church. As the head of the Chinese Mission in Singapore, the church also served as a hub where many European missionaries sojourned to acquire competence in the Chinese language before they were posted to mission fields elsewhere.

A National Monument of Singapore, religious services continue to be held daily at this church.

Architectural Features

The Church of Sts Peter and Paul is an excellent example of a traditional Neo-Gothic church. It is significantly endowed with rich detailing, ornamentation and craftsmanship. Exhibiting a rare and distinctive architectural design and approach to building planning, the church is also one of a few structures in Singapore to have rose windows with stained glass.

The church façade is characterised by a prominent spire tower and pointed arches supported by granite Corinthian capital columns. The statues of St Peter and St Paul can be seen on the second level. Just inside the main entrance is another statue of St Paul.

Church of
Sts Peter & Paul

225C Queen Street
S(188554)

CHURCH OF THE SACRED HEART

Located along Tank Road off Clemenceau Avenue, the Church of the Sacred Heart is historically linked with both the Cantonese and Hakka Catholic congregation of the Church of Sts Peter and Paul. The growth in the numbers of Cantonese and Hakka Catholics resulted in the need to fund a separate church at the turn of the 20th century.

Costing approximately $50,000, this church—the first Cantonese-Hakka Catholic church—was constructed between 1908 and 1910, and was officially opened on 11 September 1910.

Father L. Lambert of the French Mission, who was a trained architect, was responsible for the design of this church. Architecturally, this church can be said to be one-of-its-kind in Singapore. Lambert's design was believed to be inspired by the Neo-Renaissance style modelled after the 17th-century churches of Christopher Wren in London.

Within the consciousness of Singaporeans, the Church of the Sacred Heart is a landmark of Clemenceau Avenue, although this restored church building has yet to join the ranks of Singapore's national monuments at the time of writing.

Church of the
Sacred Heart

111 Tank Road
S(238069)

CIVILIAN WAR MEMORIAL AND CENOTAPH

One of the first war commemorative structures erected by the independent Singapore Government was the War Memorial in 1967. This was in response to the Imperial Japanese Army's Sook Ching ("purging of Chinese") Massacre during the early days of the Occupation that began in February 1942.

After the war, many local Chinese felt that the Japanese did not repay their 'blood debt' to the victims, and this feeling lingered on. The discovery of five war mass graves at Siglap (at the east coast of Singapore) in 1962 brought the entire matter back to the forefront. By that time, Singapore had become a self-governing state. This became a highly emotional and politicised issue; it was of great concern to Singapore's Chinese population as almost every Chinese family knew of someone who did not return from the Sook Ching screening centres.

In search of a satisfactory resolution, the government turned what was essentially a Chinese tragedy and memory of a wartime atrocity into a nation-building experience, and a collective memory for all Singaporeans. Exhumed remains of the victims were to be reburied at a national memorial. The government sought to downplay the Chinese character of the matter by promoting a Singaporean approach that included the other ethnic groups. This plan differed from Chinese expectations that a Chinese memorial would be set up in a Chinese cemetery. The Sook Ching Massacre was to be seen as suffering by all ethnic groups, and not just the Chinese alone.

The Civilian War Memorial was built at Beach Road. Its four white pillars represent the four major Singaporean ethnic groups: Chinese, Malay, Indian and Eurasian. A small inner area is formed at the base of the pillar, allowing the expression of private grief and individual commemoration of the Sook Ching victims.

Civilian War
Memorial and
Cenotaph

War Memorial Park,
Beach Road.

一九四二年二月十五日至一九四五年

八月十八日壹佰餘新嘉坡我平民無

辜死於非命不可勝計越二十餘年始

克收殮遺骸重葬於此並樹豐碑永誌悲

Cenotaph

Although Singapore was not in a theatre of war during World War I, some of its European sons volunteered to fight in the war. Eager to do their bit for the British Empire, these Singapore volunteers and their counterparts from the Malay states formed a Malayan contingent for military service in Field Marshal Kitchener's armies at the Western Front. The first contingent of volunteers sailed to Europe on 11 November 1914, marking Singapore's first-ever military involvement in a global war. These volunteers were not spared of the horrors of trench warfare and stalemate on the Western Front; 124 of them were killed in action.

The Cenotaph in Whitehall, London, is possibly the best known among the 130 or so war cemeteries and memorials in the British Commonwealth commemorating the fallen members of British and Dominion forces in World War I. Following London's example, the Straits Settlements Government also built a Cenotaph at the Esplanade seafront to honour the memory of the dead, and as a permanent record of Singapore's contribution to the Empire. This was the first state-sponsored formal military memorial in Singapore. Governor Sir Laurence Guillemard laid the foundation stone on 15 November 1920. Denis Santry of the famed architectural firm Swan & MacLaren designed Singapore's Cenotaph, which rather resembles Sir Edward Luytens' Cenotaph in Whitehall. In fact, the same inscription— 'To Our Glorious Dead'—was used in the Singapore Cenotaph.

Given the savage nature of modern war, many remains of soldiers could not be recovered for proper burial. Designed as an empty tomb, the Cenotaph was thus a symbolic tomb for every fallen soldier. This assumed a great significance for many families who lost a father, brother and son in the war.

By locating the Cenotaph at the Esplanade, adjacent to the government offices at Empress Place (now the Asian Civilisations Museum), the old Court House (now the Arts House at Old Parliament), the Padang and St Andrew's Cathedral in the heart of colonial Singapore's civic district, the government brought the war dead to the forefront of public view. The Cenotaph took on a political role in colonial Singapore as a symbol demonstrating the unity of the British Empire. During the annual commemoration of Armistice Day on 11 November, wreaths were laid, and parades were held at the adjacent Padang.

Considered a site of mourning, the Cenotaph was even co-opted to mark the passing of the Chief Scout of the World, Lord Baden-Powell of Gilwell on 18 January 1941 by the Boy Scouts and Girl Guides of Singapore. The empty tomb served as the site for the fictitious burial ceremony of this retired General of the British Army and hero of Mafeking in the Boer War who had died in Kenya on 8 January 1941.

In post-war Singapore, the Cenotaph's status as a military memorial was reinforced by the use of the reverse side to honour the World War II dead. Departing from the former practice of listing the war dead, the colonial government installed two large bronze plaques in English, Chinese, Jawi and Tamil inscriptions, which read: 'They died so we might live'. The Cenotaph continued to be used to commemorate Armistice Day in the post-World War II years, right up to Singapore's independence.

DALHOUSIE OBELISK

Along the bank of the Singapore River at Empress Place is the Dalhousie Obelisk. This is Singapore's first public monument, which was constructed to commemorate the 1850 visit of Marquis Dalhousie to Singapore. This structure was designed by John Turnbull Thomson, a government architect and surveyor, who was inspired by an Egyptian obelisk known as Cleopatra's Needle sited on the Thames Embankment in London.

Lord Dalhousie was the Governor-General of India from 1848 to 1856. Accompanied by his wife Marchioness Dalhousie, he arrived in Singapore on 17 February 1850 for a three-day visit and was welcomed by the Governor, Temenggong, European residents, Chinese merchants as well as other business leaders. As the British East India Company administered the settlement of Singapore through the Governor-General of India during this period, the objective of his visit was to consider reducing administrative expenditures.

After the visit, a series of special meetings were held to discuss how the Singapore community could express their dedication to Lord Dalhousie. The conclusion reached was to have a monument erected to commemorate the visit of the Governor-General with the placement of a historical marker on the river bank where he stepped foot. To set up the permanent memorial, Singapore residents decided on the erection of an obelisk by means of a $5 subscription fund. The Committee of the Dalhousie Testimonial comprised M.F. Davidson, J. Guthrie, Tan Kim Seng, Ang Choon Seng and Seah Eu Chin.

However, the Singapore public was not supportive on the proposed memorial for Lord Dalhousie and questioned the *raison d'être* for it. A letter in the weekly *Straits Times* issue of September 1850 questioned the need of building a monument in honour of a man "who never…did anything for the Settlement except shake hands all round with the Chamber of Commerce who in itself has yet to subscribe a penny towards a memorial fitting the father of the colony (Sir Stamford Raffles)…" Another writer shared that he "could not understand, how a nobleman who

ERECTED
BY THE EUROPEAN
CHINESE AND NATIVE
INHABITANTS OF SINGAPORE
TO COMMEMORATE THE VISIT
IN THE MONTH OF FEBRUARY 1850
OF THE MOST NOBLE
THE MARQUIS OF DALHOUSIE, K.T.
GOVERNOR GENERAL OF BRITISH INDIA
ON WHICH OCCASION
HE EMPHATICALLY RECOGNIZED
THE WISDOM OF LIBERATING COMMERCE
FROM ALL RESTRAINTS,
UNDER WHICH ENLIGHTENED POLICY
THIS SETTLEMENT HAS
RAPIDLY ATTAINED ITS PRESENT RANK
AMONG BRITISH POSSESSIONS
AND WITH WHICH
ITS FUTURE PROSPERITY MUST
EVER BE IDENTIFIED.

Dalhousie Obelisk

Empress Place

only visited Singapore for a few days and had never done anything towards its advancement or its formation should be entitled to a mark of respect such as had never been paid to its founder, the greatest man that had yet visited this quarter of the globe."

Nevertheless, towards the end of 1850, the Dalhousie Obelisk was quietly completed. This structure was first sited at Dalhousie Ghaut (which was a new jetty located at the end of High Street named in honour of the Governor-General), but was removed in 1886 for being in the way of the planned Connaught Drive as well as obstructing the construction work of the Anderson Bridge. In 1885, there were acrimonious calls for the monument to be demolished to make way for the construction of the new road and road bridge. These calls were rejected by Governor Sir Cecil Clementi on grounds that the acts of former generations of Singaporeans should not be allowed to fall into oblivion. Instead, the obelisk was dismantled and re-assembled a distance away on 9 July 1890. A year later, the obelisk was again relocated to another site near the Empress Place Building, where it has stood for over 109 years.

For the record, Lord Dalhousie's visit did not produce any tangible results for the residents of Singapore as the Governor-General gave little recognition to the port of Singapore, which merchants felt needed modern facilities to improve its efficiency. This obelisk serves only as a permanent reminder of his visit to Singapore.

EMPRESS PLACE BUILDING
(ASIAN CIVILISATIONS MUSEUM)

Walking along Boat Quay, one cannot help but notice a hive of activities taking place at a colonial building across the river; that is the Asian Civilisations Museum, occupying the Empress Place Building.

Originally known as the Government Offices, the building provided offices for the government departments located in the Maxwell House (now known as Parliament House). Amongst the various departments housed were the Secretariat, Audit Office, Registration of Deeds Office, Land Office, Public Works and Medical Department, and even the Inspector General of the Police Force.

In 1907, a public square outside the building was named Empress Place in honour of Queen Victoria. Over time, the Government Offices became associated and synonymous with Empress Place.

The Empress Place Building was constructed in four phases between 1864 and 1920 in order to provide new space for the expanding colonial government. The original section was designed by colonial engineer J.F.A. McNair, utilising convict labour for its construction. The remaining extensions were built in 1880, 1904–1909 and 1920. These subsequent additions followed the Neo-Palladian design of McNair such that the building achieved a harmonious look.

The building continued to be used by government departments until the 1980s. After the government departments vacated the building, renovation works took place to convert it into a museum. The Empress Place Museum opened in April 1989, hosting exhibitions on Chinese History. The museum was closed in April 1995, but re-opened its doors as the Asian Civilisations Museum in 2002, exhibiting Southeast, South and West Asian collections.

The Empress Place building is a National Monument, and was gazetted in February 1992.

Empress Place Building

1 Empress Place S(179555)

FORT CANNING HILL

Prior to the arrival of the British, this hill had been known as Bukit Larangan (Forbidden Hill) from the days of Temasek. It was the home of the early Malay kings, and also a burial site. The Keramat (tomb of) Iskandar Shah, who was the last of five kings mentioned in the *Sejarah Melayu* (Malay Annals), marks the remains of the old royal burial grounds. This brick structure was already present when Raffles first arrived in Singapore.

In the early days of the British settlement of Singapore, the hill was first known as Government Hill. Government Hill was also the site of the first Government House which served as the residence of Sir Stamford Raffles, and the first Christian cemetery in Singapore.

The Government House was demolished in 1857 to make way for the construction of a fort. The British Government added military fortifications and installed seven 68-pound guns at Government Hill to bolster the defences of Singapore town. The hill was thus renamed Fort Canning in honour of Viscount Charles John Canning (first viceroy of India in 1858). However, it was never used in any hostilities.

In 1907, the fort became the Singapore Base District Headquarters for the Malaya Command. The old fort was demolished in 1923, and was replaced with a series of new buildings and underground structures. The latter included a bomb-proof underground bunker comprising meeting rooms and an operations centre. It was the largest military complex in Singapore up to the 1940s. During the Japanese invasion, this structure was the command headquarters of General Arthur Percival. It was within this structure that General

Percival and his other generals made the decision to surrender Singapore to General Yamashita on 14 February 1942.

Fort Canning was then used as a command headquarters for the Japanese military during the Japanese Occupation, before being reverted to British use as the British Army Far East Command Centre in post-war Singapore. When Singapore was a part of Malaysia, the fort was the defence headquarters of the Malaysian Armed Forces stationed in Singapore. After Singapore gained independence, it was occupied by the Singapore Armed Forces (SAF), and was for a number of years the SAF's Command Staff College.

The underground bunker has been restored and is now used as a war museum known as The Battle Box. Visitors can view crafted war figurines representing General Percival and his staff having a conference and reaching the decision of surrender. The former military headquarter buildings have been adapted for new usage as The Legends Fort Canning Park, a town club. Some structures of the original 1857 fortifications at the southern slope of the hill have been restored and now forms part of Fort Caning Park.

An underground reservoir was built on the hill's summit in 1926. It remains in operation today.

Archaeology at Fort Canning

In modern, urban Singapore, many would readily dismiss a person claiming that the remains of 14th century Temasek lies beneath our feet. The founding of Temasek by Sang Nila Utama (a prince from the Javanese kingdom of Majaphahit) is considered to be nothing more than a Malay lore. However, Fort Canning is one of the few sites containing a wealth of undisturbed artefacts dating from the Temasek era.

During the 1926 construction of a service reservoir on the top of the hill, gold ornaments dating from the 14th century were excavated. These comprised finger rings, ear ornaments and an arm ornament, giving credence that an ancient settlement was based here. It was not until 1984 when proper archaeological research began with the excavation of an area north of the Keramat Iskandar Shah. Archaeologists found some 40,000 pre-colonial artefacts (such as Chinese porcelain, glass beads, porcelain and Chinese wares) laying in an undisturbed context. Some 16 Chinese coins were also been yielded from this area. The oldest coin dates from the Tang Dynasty (618–906), and the others from the Northern Song (960–1126) and Southern Song reign of Emperor Gao Zong (1127–1130).

While Fort Canning has yet to be fully excavated, the artifacts that have been found so far suggest that it was occupied as a royal centre in the first half of the 14th century. The abundance of unearthed glass globules and glass beads indicate that glass recycling was a craft activity that took place here. The site is also marked by an absence of archaeological remains between 1600 and 1800. This supports the story that Temasek had been attacked by an external party, which caused its decline and eventual demise as a flourishing port.

A permanent model of an archaeological site was set up in 2001.

Fort Canning Cemetery

This early cemetery contained the graves of European adults and children. The decision to set up a Christian cemetery was due to the high mortality rates of Europeans in the tropical environment. In those days prior to the invention of antibiotics and anti-malarial medications, overseas postings within the colonial service were deemed to be the white man's grave.

In 1834, the Christian cemetery was relocated towards another site on the hill where the Fort Canning Gateways stand today. The cemetery consisted of two sections—the southern section reserved for Anglican burials, and the northern section reserved for burials of other Christian denominations. Over time, the cemetery also accepted burials of Chinese Christians. In 1865, Fort Canning Cemetery was closed and the graves were relocated to other burial grounds.

Today, there are still a few reminders of this old cemetery. Among the most prominent are the 1846 Gothic gateways. The gateways were built to support a low hedge that defined the cemetery's perimeter. G.D. Coleman was believed to be the architect responsible for these gateways that were constructed shortly after his death in 1844. They were the earliest examples of the Gothic revival style seen in Singapore, along with St Andrew's Cathedral and St Joseph's Church.

Fort Canning Lighthouse

A flagstaff was erected in 1855 on Fort Canning. This became a lighthouse of sorts in 1903 with the affixation of a bright light signal on the flagstaff. Many ships and marine craft depended on the light for guidance when navigating into Singapore River and Keppel Harbour. A proper lighthouse was constructed on the southern side of the hill in 1903 to replace the flagstaff. Constructed by Riley, Hargreaves & Co Ltd, the lighthouse was a steel semi-skeletal 24.3-metre tower. Surmounted by a wind vane, the light shone from 61.6 metres above sea level, and had a range of 19 nautical miles.

LIM BO SENG MEMORIAL AND
INDIAN NATIONAL ARMY MEMORIAL

Prominently situated along Queen Elizabeth Walk is the Lim Bo Seng Memorial. This unique structure represents the official commemoration of a local Chinese who heroically resisted the Japanese even as the local Chinese community endured untold sufferings during the Japanese Occupation from 1942 to 1945. Lim, a Force 136 officer who died from torture while in Japanese captivity in Perak, was honoured with a special memorial unveiled on the 10th anniversary of his death on 29 June 1954.

Lim's remains were exhumed after the war and returned to Singapore. He was reburied on the grounds of MacRitchie Reservoir on 13 January 1946 with full military honours, and also posthumously promoted to Major-General by Generalissimo Chiang Kai-Shek.

The Lim Bo Seng Memorial Committee commissioned well-known Singapore architect Ng Keng Seng to design the memorial. Taking the form of a Chinese pagoda on a raised marble octagonal platform, this conical structure features a bronze roof with four bronze lions at the foot.

- Lim Bo Seng Memorial
- Queen Elizabeth Walk

Just a stone's throw away is a historic site marker in the place of the Indian National Army (INA) Memorial that was destroyed by the British in late 1945. During the war, the INA was under the leadership of Subhas Chandra Bose, who led them to fight alongside the Japanese army against the British and Allied forces in Burma. The National Heritage Board had set up this marker. Former Cabinet minister S Dhanabalan officially unveiled it on 15 July 1995.

• Indian National
Army Memorial
• Queen Elizabeth Walk

MASONIC LODGE

While the first Freemason to land on Singapore was Sir Stamford Raffles in 1819, Freemasonry would only be officially founded in Singapore in December 1845 with the establishment of Zetland Lodge No 508 E.C. in a house at Armenian Street. The first Singapore Freemason to be initiated was lawyer William Napier (who founded the law firm Drew & Napier) on 15 December 1845.

The house at Coleman Street has been the Masonic Lodge since 27 December 1879. It was designed by Thomas A Cargill, a Municipal Engineer and a Freemason. He was also the designer of Coleman Bridge and was at one time Editor of the *Straits Times*.

This 1879 building is an active home of Freemasons. The building's façade bears the iconic Masonic symbols of the square and compass. It has a basement which houses the administrative offices and Masonic library, while the restaurant, bar and kitchen occupies the ground floor. Regular Masonic meetings are held at rooms located on the second floor. Walking up the staircase to the second floor, one will see the stained glass windows and a bronze bust of William Henry Read, as well as portraits of other prominent Freemasons.

On the second floor, one will find various rooms used for the conduct of Masonic meetings and ceremonies. These include the:

- Meeting Room (West Temple): This is referred to as the small temple by Freemasons and is for ceremonial use. There are two stained glass windows that depict the Arms and Heraldry of the Irish and Scottish masons. On the walls are plaques that list the names of Masters who had headed the various orders of freemasonry since 1874.
- Member's Robing Room: The portraits of District Grand Masters since 1858 are displayed here.
- District Officers Robing Room: Photographs of annual installation meetings of various lodges as well as medal collections are displayed here.
- Candidates Robing Room: Displayed here are the framed warrants of the various lodges meeting in the Masonic Lodge.

- Main Meeting Room (Temple): Regular monthly lodge meetings are held in the Temple. There is an order in the seating arrangements which sees the Master being seated in the east while his two wardens sit in the west and south. Seated at the north are the Secretary and Treasurer. Other members such as the past Masters, Grand Lodge Officers, full masons and newly-initiated masons are assigned seats within the Temple.

Members of the public are allowed to dine at the ground floor restaurant. Guided tours are to be arranged in advance with the Masonic Lodge.

The Masonic Lodge is a gazetted conservation building.

Masonic Lodge
23A Coleman Street
S(179806)

MICA BUILDING
(FORMER HILL STREET POLICE STATION)

Prominently located at the corner of Hill Street and River Valley Road is the former Hill Street Police Station. Designed by F. Dorrington in Classical Renaissance architectural style, this six-storey building was one of the tallest buildings and the most modern police facility in Singapore then in 1934. It was briefly renamed Silver Jubilee Building to commemorate the 25th anniversary of the reign of King George V in 1935.

The building had offices for the police as well as supporting services that included garages for police vehicles, police barracks and even living quarters for married policemen and their families. The Singapore Police was based here for 46 years until vacating the premises in 1980.

Renamed Hill Street Building in 1983, this government building housed various departments such as the Oral History Department, Offices of the Official Assignee and the Film Censors until 1997.

A gazetted National Monument since 1998, the building was restored and refurbished in the late 1990s for its new role as the Ministry of Information and the Arts (MITA). While the building's Shanghai plaster façade along Hill Street and River Valley Road was retained, physical changes to the building involved the demolition of the old toilet block and an accommodation block. This provided new space for the creation of a driveway behind the building. A new basement was created below the courtyard of the building for car park and plant facilities.

Other changes within the building involved the introduction of a glass roof to cover the open veranda, which used to be a police parade ground. This was necessary to maintain a centralised air-conditioned environment. The atrium is now used as a venue for art exhibitions, performance and events. A modern life lobby was also added to the premises.

The external façade was modified with the use of eye-catching colours for its wooden window shutters. Painted in blue, yellow and pink, these colourful windows brighten the mood of the former police station.

The building was officially named MITA Building in November 2000, and renamed MICA Building in the early 2000s. This building now houses the Ministry of Information, Communications and the Arts (MICA), Singapore Kindness Movement, Media Development Authority, National Arts Council and other statutory bodies.

MIDDLE ROAD CHURCH (Sculpture Square)

At the junction of Middle Road and Waterloo Street is a small, single-storey church-like building. Popularly known as Sculpture Square in recent years, this 1875 building is amongst the few structures from the 19th century that remains in the Middle Road area.

Constructed for use by Mr C. Phillips to advance the spread of the gospel to Eurasians, this building was first known as the Christian Institute. In the early days, it was also used as a girls' day school under the management of Miss Sophia Blackmore from the Woman's Foreign Missionary Society of the Methodist Episcopal Church. The church was popularly known as the Malay Church due to the religious ceremonies conducted in vernacular Malay language for the Straits-born Chinese (known as the Baba) congregation, and this marked the first beginnings of the Straits Chinese church. Malay-language Christian services were held there under Reverend W.G. Shellabear beginning 1894.

However, missionary work was also conducted from this building to reach out to the Chinese of other dialects. In 1894, the Foochow Chinese Mission began its work from this building under the leadership of Dr Luering. So successful was the work of the

Methodist Church that in 1900 it acquired the property from the Women's Foreign Missionary Society.

In 1901, Methodist Bishop F.W. Warne officiated the dedication of this building as the Middle Road Church. The Baba Church, as it was also known, grew to a point where the building was deemed insufficient for the large congregation. Following the sale of the property to Mr Eu Tong Sen in 1926, the Baba Church moved to its new premises in Kampong Kapor Methodist Church in 1929.

With the vacating of the Baba Church, this building was converted into commercial use. It functioned as a car garage by Sin Sin Motor Company until the late 1980s. In the early 2000s, the building was restored and converted into an art exhibition hall.

Middle Road Church

155 Middle Road
S(188977)

MONUMENT TO THE EARLY FOUNDERS OF SINGAPORE

Hardly anyone is aware that a commemorative structure was once sited at Collyer Quay, facing the sea; based there for a three-decade period was a monument to the pioneers of Singapore.

On 18 January 1970, President Yusof Ishak officially unveiled the foundation stone for what was called the Singapore Monument. During the formative years of the Republic of Singapore, this commemorative structure was to serve as a reminder to future generations of this city-state that the greatest contributions towards the achievements of Singapore were the work of all its early founders and immigrants.

The foundation stone of the Singapore Monument features a very simple design constructed with basic building materials. The base comprises a red brick platform that steeply rises like a miniature Mayan pyramid. A rectangular granite block crowns the summit of this brick structure. This four-cornered structure symbolises the arrival of immigrants to Singapore from the four geographical corners of the globe.

Each of the four sides of the granite block bears an inscription that pays tribute to the early pioneers of Singapore in the languages of Malay, Chinese, Tamil and English. The English text reads:

> This Foundation Stone of the Monument in tribute
> to The Early Founders of Singapore was laid by
> Inche Yusof Ishak The President of the Republic of
> Singapore on the 18th day of January 1970

However, no visible follow-up was done to erect a proper Singapore Monument. Over time, the foundation stone became the de facto Monument to The Early Founders of Singapore.

While this structure was meant to be a monument, it became viewed as a hindrance to be removed in the late 1990s, when Collyer Quay was identified for redevelopment. Amongst the improvement works scheduled was the widening of the roads. The Singapore Monument's location had obstructed the path of development and it

Monument to the
Early Founders
of Singapore
1 Canning Rise
S(179868)

was initially slated for demolition. The Singapore Monument had no legal status of having been gazetted as a National Monument. As it enjoyed no protection under the Monuments legislation, there was no compliance for any institution to see to its retention.

However, the proposed demolition did not take place due to the intervention of Ms Uma Devi, Senior Assistant Director of the Historic Sites Unit, National Heritage Board. Recognising the significance of this simple structure, she attended to the physical dismantling of the structure, securing a new location for it, and its eventual re-assembly. Since then, the structure has stood quietly in a small garden lining the driveway of the National Archives Building.

MPH BUILDING

Located at the juncture of Stamford Road and Armenian Street is a century-old building many still remember fondly as MPH. Now used as a furniture showroom, this iconic building occupied a special place in the hearts of many people in Singapore and Malaysia for many decades, and is an integral part of the social memory and fabric of Singapore.

The two-storey building features Edwardian commercial street architecture of the 1900–1910 period. It has an elaborately modelled façade consisting of Italian cinquecento (pedimented and arched windows, rusticated piers) and bold baroque arches, supported by the first-storey arcade. It is one of a handful of very rare Singapore buildings of the Edwardian era that remains in Singapore.

MPH was one of the first indigenous book stores of Singapore. For nine decades since 1908, it was one of the oldest commercial tenants to be found along Stamford Road and Armenian Street.

The MPH Building had played an important role in the history of Singapore and Malaysia. It helped in facilitating the growth of two institutions—the Methodist Church and the Boy Scout Movement. It also produced a variety of early Malayan publications, such as *Hikayat Abdullah* (Autobiography of Munshi Abdullah), *Sejarah Melayu* (The Malay Annals), *The Legal Status of the Malay States*, *A Practical Malay Grammar*, *Geography of British Malaya* and other classic books.

MPH's roots can be traced back to 1815 when a young missionary, William Milne, chose Malacca to establish a permanent mission press. This eventually led to the setting up of the Amelia Bishop Press in Singapore in 1890 by Captain William G. Shellabear, with the aim of printing Christian literature. In 1893, the mission press moved to Raffles Place in Singapore and its name was changed to the American Mission Press. Reverend William T. Cherry then turned this mission press into a multi-faceted organisation, diversifying into printing, publishing and book distribution. In 1906, its name was changed to the Methodist Publishing House.

The origins of the building came about in 1907 when the Methodist Church decided to construct a place for the Methodist Publishing House at Stamford Road. Work quickly commenced after local architecture firm Swan & MacLaren drew up the plans. The building was completed in 1908, and MPH commenced operations here.

MPH was responsible for publishing many religious tracts, hymn books and the Bible translated in Malay, Chinese and other vernacular languages for use in spreading the gospel. In working with the Bible Society located along Armenian Street, MPH helped to advance the gospel in Southeast Asia. Amongst the first commercial business ventures of the Methodist Church, MPH was very profitable and the church enjoyed success as a publisher. However, this also posed great problems to the Methodist Church, and it divested the company in 1928. MPH was incorporated as Malaya Publishing House when it became a public stock company. Frank Cooper Sands purchased the company and became its Managing Director.

Quickly becoming a leading book company in Singapore and Malaysia, MPH was one of the first local enterprises to become a

MPH Building
71-77 Stamford Road, S(178895)

regional player in the publishing industry. Through the years, MPH underwent several revisions to its name to reflect the changes in its ownership—Malaya Publishing House (1928), Malaysia Publishing House (1963), MPH Limited (1968), Jack-Chia MPH (1972) and MPH Limited (1999). However, its acronym remained constant throughout the years. MPH Building was sold by MPH Limited in 2002 and it ceased to be the flagship book shop for the company ever since.

The MPH was also the unofficial headquarters for the Scout Movement in Singapore and the Malay Peninsula during the period between 1910 and 1956, while Frank Cooper Sands was working there. A long-time employee, Sands' 48-year career from 1910 to 1958 accorded him complete control of the firm, which he used to advance the cause of the Boy Scout Movement. MPH Building was the de facto nerve centre of the Singapore and British Malayan Boy Scout Movement from 1910 to 1949. He used the MPH printing facilities to publish local Scouting literature and tapped the MPH book distribution network to supply schools throughout the Malay states with Scouting books, badges, uniform and equipment. MPH also functioned as a Boy Scout uniform and equipment supplies shop for Singapore and Malayan Boy Scouts from the 1920s until the 1960s.

Frank Cooper Sands was the highest-ranking Boy Scout official in Malaya from 1920 to 1949. The Boy Scout Associations of both countries acknowledge him as the Father of Singapore and Malaysian Scouting, having promoted the growth and entrenchment of the Boy Scout movement in Singapore and Malaya during its infant years.

OLD SUPREME COURT AND CITY HALL

Facing the Padang and the sea, the Old Supreme Court building is amongst one of the best-designed British colonial Neo-Classical buildings in Singapore. Based on the site of the former Grand Hotel de L'Europe, it was constructed between 1937 and 1939 at a cost of 1.75 million British Straits Settlements dollars, based on the architectural design of Frank Dorrington Ward (Chief Architect of Public Works Department). Sir Thomas Shenton Whitelegge Thomas, Governor of the Straits Settlements, declared the building open and handed it over to the then Chief Justice, Sir Percy McElwaine, on 3 August 1939.

The Old Supreme Court consists of four wings surrounded by a central courtyard capped by a dome that exploits natural light to illuminate the space. As one enters the building, one will notice that the ground-floor lobby is characterised by a large octagonal foundation stone. This stone, measuring seven feet across and weighing two tons, was laid by Sir Shenton Thomas, Governor of the Straits Settlements on 1 April 1937. This coincided with the 70th anniversary of the Straits Settlements as a British Colony, separate from British India. Underneath the foundation stone is buried a time capsule containing six Singapore newspapers from 31 March 1937 and some Straits Settlement coins. The time capsule is scheduled for retrieval in the year 3000!

Prior to the Supreme Court moving to its new building in 2005, the Old Supreme Court building housed eight courtrooms with adjoining Judges' Chambers. Due to the increasing load on the Supreme Court, in November 1986 Chief Justice Wee Chong Jin gave directions for the construction of 12 additional courtrooms in the neighbouring City Hall building, which had previously been allocated to the Supreme Court by the Prime Minister's Office. Extensive renovations took place in the City Hall building between November 1987 and May 1991. In June 1991, the Supreme Court Registry and Library moved to the City Hall building. Other occupants of the building included the Public Service Commission and the Industrial Arbitration Court.

While City Hall's association with the Supreme Court is brief, the building has been a witness of many historical events. Constructed from 1926 to 1929 for use as the Municipal Building, it housed all the major departments of the Singapore Municipality. Designed by municipal architect F.D. Meadows, the Municipal Building's façade was dominated by 18 large Corinthian columns (which were the work of Cavalieri Rudolfo Nolli). The columns and the building's steps became Singapore's prominent public spaces.

This building was where Admiral Lord Louis Mountbatten accepted the surrender of all Japanese forces in Southeast Asia on 12 September 1945. The signing of the surrender document was held in the Municipal Building's chamber, while the formal ceremony took place on its steps.

Old Supreme
Court and
City Hall

1 St Andrew's Road
S(178957)

Following the proclamation of Singapore as a city in 1951, the building was renamed City Hall. It served as the Prime Minister's Office, Ministry of Foreign Affairs and Ministry of Culture during the early days of the Republic of Singapore. Singapore's first Prime Minister Lee Kuan Yew and members of his Cabinet were sworn into office on 5 June 1959 at the City Hall Chamber. Similarly, the second Prime Minister Goh Chok Tong and the Cabinet took their Oaths of Allegiance and Oaths of Office in the chamber in November 1990. The City Hall steps have also been where the President, Prime Minister, Cabinet ministers and Members of Parliament reviewed the National Day Parade.

The Old Supreme Court and City Hall buildings are National Monuments of Singapore. As part of Singapore's aspirations to become a global arts city, the Singapore Government has announced plans to convert these buildings into the National Art Gallery. Following participation by a number of leading architectural firms in

a design competition, the government appointed French firm Studio Milou Architecture to undertake the work to create the art gallery.

Architectural Features of Old Supreme Court

Amongst the best-known features of the former Supreme Court building is the tympanum, featuring sculpture reliefs that fit into the enclosed space. Originating from Classical Greek architecture, the pediment and tympanum formed the façade of Greek temples, as seen in the Parthenon in Athens.

Weighing approximately 13 tons, the former Supreme Court's tympanum is 36 feet long and approximately nine feet in height at its apex. The reliefs on the tympanum were done by Italian sculptor Cavalieri Rudolfo Nolli.

The allegory of Justice is located prominently in the centre of the sculpted tympanum. Seated on a throne, the allegory of Justice holds the scales of justice on the right hand and a sword on the left. Nolli

had integrated the characteristics of Greek Goddess Themis and Roman Goddess Justicia in his sculpture of the allegory of Justice.

While the phrase "Justice is blind" is familiar to many people and the allegory of Justice is often represented as blindfolded, Lady Justice in Singapore has her eyes wide open in the administration of justice. On its right side (represented by the scales), justice is administered and the wrong-doer is punished while on the left (represented by the sword), proper administration of law and justice brings about prosperity and joy.

Surrounding the allegory of Justice are other figures that contribute to the tympanum sculpture. Seen from the street view, a seated man is bitten by a multi-headed snake (symbolising a lost soul) followed by a scribe writing onto a scroll under the view of a standing man holding a bound manuscript in his hands (symbolising the legislation of law). Adjacent to the throne of the allegory of Justice is a kneeling woman begging for justice. On the other side of the throne is a woman with her head bowed in submission, followed by a man with a magnificent bull and two children holding an abundant harvest of wheat. These figurines symbolise the fruits (prosperity and joy) to be enjoyed when justice is administered.

Sculptures are not confined only to the tympanum of this building. There are also five bas relief panels located above the main porch. Measuring nine feet long and two feet wide, each of these panels illustrate life in British colonial Singapore. Beginning from the side panel facing High Street, the construction of the Supreme Court Building is depicted. Chinese coolies are busy at work while European architects and engineers pore over the building plans on a table at the construction site.

Life on a rubber plantation is represented on the second panel. Indian rubber tappers harvest the raw liquid rubber, while other Indian workers process the rubber. As rubber was one of the major cash crops of Malaya, this scene highlights the importance of this economic activity within the export economy of British Malaya. The middle of the five panels projects the beginnings of British presence in Singapore and Malaya with the signing of the 1819 treaty between Sir Stamford Raffles and the Temenggong of Singapore. Interestingly, an Indian Sepoy observes the whole proceedings while standing guard.

A Malay fishing village is romantically depicted in the fourth panel. Malay fishermen are portrayed in their daily work, netting fish in the seas, harvesting their catch and repairing fishing nets. The last panel is a depiction of international maritime trade, which is the raison d'etre for British Singapore and Malaya. Chinese and Arabic traders are engaged in negotiations, while Chinese coolies load goods onto ships. This panel pays tribute to the role played by international commerce in contributing to the growth and prosperity of Singapore.

The architecture of the Old Supreme Court building is accentuated with the bank of columns lining its façade. Comprising a mix of both Ionic and Corinthian columns, these collectively contribute to the Neo-Classical character of the building.

Supporting the tympanum are six Corinthian columns. These ornate structures are marked with elaborate capitals featuring acanthus leaves that surround the circular capital at the apex. The Ionic columns are located within the two sides of the tympanum. These differ from the former in that the capitals are characterised by volutes that form a scroll-like effects on two ends.

The dome of the building is a familiar sight in the Singapore skyline. A copper-coloured grand structure with alternating Corinthian columns and niche resses, this structure is said to bear a close resemblance to St Paul's Cathedral in London. However, visitors to the building would not be able to look at the dome's interior as it is not the building's focal point and does not feature exquisite architecture. Comprising a framework of steel trusses located on the upper storeys of the building, the dome's interior is sealed off and hidden away from public viewing.

There is a smaller dome located within the building, which is hardly known to the general public as it is not visible from the street view. Located within the central courtyard of the building, the dome's exterior is simple, and provides no hint of its elaborate interior design. Within the rotunda, this area was originally used as a legal library. The interior boasts of a triple-volume space with a single-storey floor surrounded by a circle of Corinthian columns. Sunlight pours through the windows located within the base of the circular dome.

PADANG

Located in the heart of Singapore's civic district is the Padang. Many would have passed by this open green field numerous times, witnessing the National Day parades, sporting and historical events that had taken place here over the years. Sited on the eastern and western corners of this field are the Singapore Recreation Club (SRC) and Singapore Cricket Club (SCC).

Since it was zoned for use as a playing field in 1820 (known simply as the Plain), the Padang has remained undisturbed by major construction for almost 190 years. This had not been what Stamford Raffles originally planned; he envisaged its development for use by the public, government and military. Colonel William Farquhar, Singapore's First Resident, ignored Raffles' instructions and instead reserved it as a public open space. In 1830 and 1850, developmental pressures were applied on acquiring the Padang, only to be defeated by public appeals for its retention as an open field.

The Padang is also a time capsule of Singapore's archaeological remains spanning for seven centuries since the 14th century. Excavations undertaken at test pits in the western corner of the Padang (along the SCC) in 2003 had unearthed a wealth of

artefacts that shed light on life in Temasek. The recovered artefacts included pottery and earthenware fragments from imported Chinese ceramics, Siamese Sawankhalok pottery, Vietnamese blue and white ware, metal slag, glass beads and bangles, mixed currencies from Chinese Song, Yuan, Ming and Qing Dynasties, as well as Javanese, Melaka, Sri Lankan, Portuguese and British Indian coins. The existence of multiple foreign currencies and coinage demonstrates the "international" nature of the early Temasek port, in which a sophisticated currency system was already in place to facilitate intra-regional commerce.

Singapore Recreation Club (SRC)

The SRC was founded as a sports club by the Eurasian community in 1883. It first functioned from a building at Waterloo Street before getting its permanent clubhouse at the eastern corner of the Padang on 23 June 1885. For over a century, the SRC became a focal point for the Eurasian community's social and recreational activities; the club provided many Eurasians with opportunities to participate and compete in team sports against the other clubs.

During the Japanese Occupation, the clubhouse was requisitioned for use as an outpatient clinic. After the war, SRC quickly got back on its feet under the presidency of Dr Charles Joseph Pemberton Paglar (1946–1954), and regained its place as a premier sports and social club. Under the subsequent presidency of Sir George Edward Noel Oehlers (1955–1965), SRC opened its membership to non-Eurasians, a practice that has continued to present times.

Singapore Cricket Club (SCC)

While cricket was said to have been played on the Padang since 1837, the SCC was founded in 1852. Its clubhouse, constructed in 1884, is the club's third clubhouse, and a landmark within the civic district. (Earlier clubhouses were constructed in 1860 and 1877.) The building was first extended in 1907, with the wings added in 1922.

As one of the premier clubs of Singapore in colonial era, SCC's past presidents included several governors of the then Straits

Padang

St Andrew's Road

Settlement: Sir Cecil Clementi Smith (SCC President, 1883; Governor, 1887–1893), Sir Frank Athelstane Swettenham (SCC President, 1902–1903; Governor, 1901–1903) and Sir Arthur Henderson Young (SCC President, 1909–1910; Governor, 1911–1919).

For almost a century, the SCC membership consisted of male Europeans only. In the post-war period, membership was open to people of all nationalities. Women were eligible for full membership in 1996.

A private members-only club, SCC offers other sports besides cricket. Members enjoy rugby, soccer, field hockey, squash, tennis, lawn bowls, billiards and snooker. The club is also host to the prestigious Singapore Cricket Club International Rugby Sevens tournament.

The club offers a wide food and beverage selection, and is a popular watering hole for lawyers and professionals working in Shenton Way and the Central Business District.

PERANAKAN MUSEUM (FORMER TAO NAN SCHOOL)

One of Singapore's newest museum is the Peranakan Museum. It is housed in a century-old building, which was formerly the Tao Nan School, a Chinese school established by the Hokkien community.

During the British colonial period, the colonial government only provided education in English and Malay. Chinese and Tamil vernacular education were the responsibilities of their respective communities. Hence, the clan associations provided Chinese education by setting up schools. This was also the case for Tao Nan School. On 8 November 1906, the Singapore Hokkien Huay Kuan founded the Daonan Xuetang. Its founding was mooted by Tan Kah Kee, who led the fund-raising for its construction. Prominent businessmen, such as Oei Tiong Ham who donated $10,000 towards the project, ensured that the school became a reality. The result was a modern school building with French Renaissance architectural features. Similar to the Raffles Hotel's design, it is one of the few buildings in Singapore to feature two hexagonal wings. The building was completed in 1912, and the school renamed Daonan Xuexiao (Tao Nan School).

An all-boys school, the first intake of students amounted to 90 students. This new Chinese school ushered in a new approach to Chinese education. Although it was set up with the support of the Hokkien community, the school opened its doors to all Chinese children from different dialect and provincial backgrounds. Furthermore, the school's medium of instruction was Mandarin. This was a departure from the norm of Hokkien schools teaching in the vernacular dialect of Hokkien. Tao Nan offered a comprehensive curriculum; students not only learnt the classics, but were also taught subjects such as mathematics, science, singing and physical education. In 1914, English lessons were conducted.

Peranakan Museum

39 Armenian Street
S(179941)

During World War II, the school was closed, and the premises occupied by the Japanese Army. After the Japanese surrendered in October 1945, Tao Nan School opened its doors to female students and became a co-ed school. In 1958, it became a government school, and accepted government grants and funds.

Singapore experienced rapid economic development and restructuring after independence, resulting in a shift in population demography that saw many people moving to new residential districts and housing estates. This caused the student population of Tao Nan School to be reduced significantly. In 1975, the School Management Committee, under the sponsorship of the Singapore Hokkien Huay Kuan, decided to build a new school building in Marine Parade. The building was completed in December 1981. It began functioning in 1982 with 28 classes of transferred pupils from neighbouring schools. The medium of instruction was changed, this time to English, in order to accommodate the needs of modernised Singapore.

The vacated building was taken over by the National Heritage Board, and converted into a museum with the latest facilities, which was opened in 1994. It was also gazetted as a National Monument.

RAFFLES HOTEL

The Raffles Hotel and its signature Singapore Sling cocktail drink rank amongst the best-known international tourism icons branding Singapore. The hotel first opened its doors in 1887 under the management of four Armenian brothers—Martin, Tigran, Aviet and Arshak Sarkies. They had leased a 10-room beachfront house from Syed Mohamed Alsagoff and converted it into a hotel. The building was designed by Regent Alfred John Bidwell of Swan & MacLaren.

The popularity of the hotel saw the expansion of its premises over the ensuing years. These included the addition of a pair of two-storey wings in 1890, the opening of Palm Court wing in 1894, and the opening of the three-storey Main Building in 1899, complete with electrical fittings. In 1904, the hotel opened the Bras Basah wing with 112 suites and a row of ground-floor shops. This expansion resulted in Raffles Hotel being the largest hotel within the Straits Settlements then.

The Sarkies brothers were later hit hard by the Great Depression, and went bankrupt in 1931. However, the hotel's financial problems were subsequently resolved, and a public company known as Raffles Hotel Ltd was established.

During the Japanese Occupation between 1942 and 1945, the hotel was renamed Syonan Ryokan (Syonan Inn), and was popular with the Japanese. In 1961, Malayan Banking acquired the hotel from the Alsagoff family for $1.415 million. The Overseas Chinese Banking Corporation (OCBC) also had a stake when its managing director Tan Chin Tuan acquired the Straits Trading, which had shares in the hotel. In 1972, the hotel was sold to the Development Bank of Singapore (DBS).

Following the Singapore government's gazette of Raffles Hotel as a National Monument, the hotel underwent a $160-million restoration project between 1989 and 1991. The hotel further experienced an expansion with the addition of new structures for use as restaurants, a shopping arcade, a theatre and underground car park facilities.

In 2005, Raffles Hotel (along with hotels under the Raffles Holdings chain) was acquired by Colony Capital, a US-based investment group, for $1.72 billion. The group later merged with Fairmont Hotels & Resorts to form Fairmont Raffles Hotel International.

Raffles Hotel
1 Beach Road
S(189673)

ST ANDREW'S CATHEDRAL

Named after the patron saint of Scotland, St Andrew's Cathedral is Singapore's oldest Anglican church building. It is built on grounds provided by Sir Stamford Raffles in the 1822 Singapore town plan. An earlier St Andrew's Church building was sited on this area between 1838 and 1852. However, it was considered to be structurally unsound, and was demolished after suffering two lightning strikes on the church steeple in 1845 and 1849. The current St Andrew's Cathedral was designed by Lt-Colonel Ronald MacPherson of the Madras Artillery. It was built from 1856 to 1864 with the use of Indian convict labour and under the supervision of Captain J.F.A. McNair, Colonial Engineer and Superintendent of Convicts.

The cathedral's appearance was inspired by a 13th-century Gothic Cistercian abbey called Netley, located in Hampshire, England. Departing from the flamboyant Gothic church architecture, Colonel MacPherson designed this church with clean, simple lines. Absent were the ornate decorations and elaborate tracery associated with Gothic church architecture.

Colonel MacPherson is commemorated within the church grounds, where a memorial with the Maltese cross is sited at the southern corner of the church. Other memorials can be seen within the church itself. These take the form of stained glass windows and tablets. One can find stained glass windows commemorating Stamford Raffles, John Crawfurd and Major-General William J. Butterworth. The plaque memorials commemorate the victims of the 1915 Sepoy Mutiny, along with others.

St Andrew's Cathedral has undergone a few phases of expansion. In 1952, the War Memorial Wing was added with the extension of the North Wing facing North Bridge Road. The South Transept facing the Padang was extended in 1983. In 2005, the church expanded its facilities underground. The grounds alongside North Bridge Road were excavated and construction work took place to build a new underground auditorium for the Cathedral's use. Landscaping works then took place to restore the open lawn environment.

Prior to the excavation, an intensive archaeological dig from 15 September 2003 to 10 April 2004 on the grounds facing North Bridge Road unearthed some 300,000 artefacts. Among these were British colonial-era artefacts such as 19th century coins, military badges and buttons, glass, metal, ceramics, and World War II vintage small arms ammunition.

The archaeological works further uncovered undisturbed remains from 14th century Temasek within the church's compound. These included imported porcelain and stoneware from China, locally-manufactured earthenware, glass beads and bangles, worked stone, and Chinese coinage of the Song and Yuan Dynasties. Five intact stoneware vessels, along with several porcelain celadon jarlets, were recovered as well. Other unique artefacts discovered included a 13th century Sri Lankan coin and a carved stone human head. The finds demonstrated that a large archaeological reservoir from the 14th century is present below the ground. Some of these excavated artefacts are placed on permanent display at the visitor centre facing North Bridge Road.

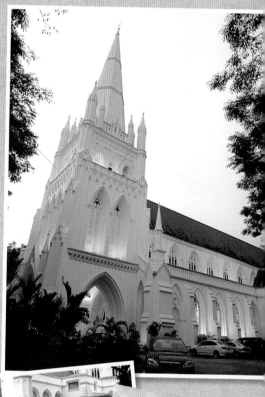

St Andrew's Cathedral

11 Saint Andrew's Road S(178959)

ST JOSEPH'S CHURCH

Facing Victoria Street is a Gothic church known as St Joseph's Church. With a history dating back to 1850, this Portuguese-Eurasian Catholic church was founded to serve the religious needs of Christians who settled in Singapore during the early days of the port of Singapore.

According to *The Portuguese Mission in Malacca and Singapore*, there were about 12 to 13 Portuguese Catholics in Singapore by 1821. While land was provided by Sir Stamford Raffles to the Catholics to build a church then, it was not until 1840 that a Catholic chapel was constructed at this site.

The current church building is located on the site of a previous St Joseph's Church (1850–1906). Architecture firm Swan & MacLaren was responsible for its design, while the firm of Riley Hargreaves oversaw construction. The foundation stone was laid in 1904, and the new church was officially opened on 30 June 1912. This phase of expansion also witnessed the construction of a new presbytery (priest house). The old parochial home was converted into a girls' school—St Anthony's Convent.

For many years, St Joseph's Church also provided for the education of children living in the neighbourhood. Beginning in 1879, a co-educational school (known as St Anna's School) was founded by Father Jose Pedro Sta Anna de Cunha in a home at Middle Road. By 1886, the fledging school had moved to a new building within the church compound. This new addition was supported with a government contribution of $4,000. St Anna's School was renamed St Anthony's Boys and Girls School. By 1893, the school had been divided into St Anthony's Boys School and St Anthony's Girls School.

St Joseph's Church was gazetted as a National Monument in 2005.

Architectural Features

The church displays traditional Gothic church architecture. Exhibiting barrel-vault construction methodology, the building has good exterior and interior composition of detailed ornamentation and craftsmanship. This is seen in the octagonal tower and spire, which are capped with a dome and flanked by two smaller towers. The Neo-Gothic style is further accentuated by the spatial quality and the use of stained glass at the windows. Portuguese ceramic tiles can be seen on the wall, sculpture and floor.

St Joseph's Church

143 Victoria Street
S(188020)

SINGAPORE ART MUSEUM
(OLD ST JOSEPH'S INSTITUTION)

This building came into existence 1855 as a Catholic boys' school known as St John's Institution, which was administered by Father Jean-Marie Beurel. A French Catholic priest, Father Beurel devoted his life to advance Catholic education in the Far East. The fledging Catholic school was renamed St Joseph's Institution at the laying of the foundation stone on 19 March 1855 (coinciding with the Feast of St Joseph).

The school quickly became Singapore's premier Catholic boys' school and experienced growth in student population over the succeeding decades. By 1906, new additions of wings were added to the original school building by Father Nain (a priest who had architectural training) to cater to the increasing student enrollment. These wings were characterised by an outward curve forming a semi-circular shape in a baroque style, matching the existing architecture language of the old central block. He also added a monumental doorway flanked by two tiers of fluted columns surmounted by a hood. The belfry was replaced with a larger dome to synchronise with the new building façade.

During the Japanese Occupation, the building continued functioning, albeit as the Bras Basah Boys' School. In post-war Singapore, the school re-opened as St Joseph's Institution. Four decades later, the school relocated to new premises at Malcolm Road as the then 130-year-old building could no longer support the expanding student population.

The vacant building was subsequently taken over by the National Heritage Board. It was restored at a cost of some $30 million for conversion into the Singapore Art Museum. This involved the addition of full climate control to allow the safe display and storage of art pieces. Since 1996, the building has enjoyed a new lease of life as the pre-eminent Singapore venue for the display of modern and contemporary Singaporean, Southeast Asian and international art.

This restored building is a National Monument of Singapore.

SINGAPORE VOLUNTEER CORPS MEMORIAL

A little-known local war memorial is the Singapore Volunteer Corps (SVC) memorial, located across the road from the Raffles Hotel. It is the only World War II memorial solely dedicated to all local Singapore volunteer soldiers who perished in the defence of Singapore or in Japanese captivity. Many SVC soldiers had become prisoners-of-war (POWs) after the British surrender. Along with British, Australian, Indian and other Allied POWs, they were used as forced labour to construct a Japanese railway line linking Thailand with Burma. Many died building the Death Railway, as it became known, and are now buried at the Kanchanaburi War Cemetery in Thailand.

- Singapore Volunteer Corps Memorial
- Former Beach Road Camp, Beach Road

Following British military tradition, the memorial was set up within the SVC's headquarters. Mounted on the exterior wall of the old SVC Drill Hall building, this modest, mounted brass plaque memorial was unveiled by Singapore Colonial Secretary Wilfred Lawson Blythe on 21 December 1950.

Since then, the memorial was maintained by soldiers of the SVC and its successor, the People's Defence Force (PDF). With the closure of the Beach Road army camp in 2000, the 2nd PDF moved to its new camp at Clementi, where it erected a replica to commemorate these SVC soldiers. The original SVC memorial remains at Beach Road.

The old SVC headquarters and other buildings in this former military camp are conservation buildings.

TAN KIM SENG FOUNTAIN

Along one corner of Queen Elizabeth Walk is a Victorian-style fountain that seems out of place with the various war commemorative structures lining the southern stretch of this road. This is the Tan Kim Seng Fountain—a 127-year-old memorial built by the Singapore municipal government in appreciation of Tan's generous donation towards the costs of early waterworks in Singapore.

The selected cast iron fountain was supplied by Messrs Andrew Handyside & Co Britannia Iron Works, Derby, and shipped to Singapore for assembly by the Municipal Engineer. It was officially dedicated to the memory of Tan Kim Seng on 19 May 1882 by Singapore Municipal President Mr Thos Scott.

Local newspapers of the day reported this event widely. The *Straits Times Overland Journal* described the fountain's design and workings in great detail:

"...the fountain's lower part consists of four panels or divisions with small pedestals dividing them from each other and forming projecting corners. Each panel is composed of a couple of cupids, sitting and leaning each an arm upon an inverted urn, the body of which is recessed in the panel, and holding in the other hand a

Tan Kim Seng
Fountain

Esplanade Park,
Queen Elizabeth Walk

trident. In front of the two cupids is placed a large shell on the edge of which their feet are resting, the shell being filled with water falling from the projecting mouth of the inverted urn already mentioned.

"Upon each of the pedestals forming, so to speak the corners of the fountain, is placed a cupid pouring water into the large concrete basin below, from an urn which he holds between his feet and tilts slightly forward as he grasps it with both hands. A circular basin of smaller dimensions than the one below surmounts the lower portion of the fountain already described and receives its supply of water from the various orifices placed in the body and upper parts of the fountain. The overflow from this basin is provided for by the addition of four oval lion heads, through which the water finds its way to the basin below.

"The main body of the fountain consists of two tiers or divisions. The lower portion of the same, so far as the pedestals are concerned is somewhat similar to the base, as it consists four panels and four pedestals, with the difference that the panels are filled with heads representing marine deities. The upper tier, forming what may be called the shaft of the fountain, is a very handsome piece of work composed for four draped female figures of an emblematical design. These are placed in a sitting posture in four niches corresponding to the four panels of the fountain. The shaft is surmounted by another circular basin of dimensions still smaller than the last mentioned one, and ornamented in a similar manner. In the centre of the basin stands a small column carrying heads of four dolphins, which support an ornamental vase, perforated in four places so as to allow water to fall into the basin beneath. From the mouth of this vase, which constitutes the summit of the fountain, the water is thrown to a height of 15 feet."

The fountain was sited at Fullerton Square until 1925, when it had to be relocated to accommodate the construction of the Fullerton Building. The structure has been sited at its present spot in the Esplanade between Queen Elizabeth Walk and Connaught Drive ever since. Despite requiring restoration work, this fountain is still in working condition.

TAN KIM SENG (1805–1864)

A Straits-born Chinese merchant from Malacca, Tan Kim Seng is one of the early pioneers of Singapore. In 1840 he set up the trading firm Kim Seng & Company, and enjoyed success in his entrepreneur endeavors. As a Chinese community leader and a Justice of the Peace, he was the second Asian after Tan Seng Poh to be appointed a member of the Municipal Commission in 1857.

Tan was a charitable man who supported many philanthropic causes of the day, including the Chinese Free School and Tan Tock Seng Hospital. He also provided $13,000 towards the construction of Singapore's first public waterworks for the supply of fresh water to inhabitants of Singapore town in 1857. He proposed the supply of piped water from Bukit Timah to Singapore town. However, nothing of note was put into effect by the Singapore Municipality into improving the supply and distribution of water; it had been said that the Municipality squandered away the donation. It was only some 21 years later that the Singapore Municipality realised Tan's vision with the creation of an impounding reservoir.

In 1882 the Singapore Municipality erected the Tan Kim Seng Fountain in commemoration of Tan's generous donation (and also partly out of shame at having mishandled the project for two decades). The choice of a fountain is a direct association with Tan's motivations to provide the public with flowing water.

Tan Kim Seng is also remembered in Singapore with Kim Seng Road (linking River Valley Road to Havelock Road) and Kim Seng Bridge.

VICTORIA THEATRE AND CONCERT HALL

The Victoria Theatre and Concert Hall are historical landmarks of Singapore's cityscape. Often seen as one building, there are actually two buildings constructed 45 years apart—one during the mid-19th century, and the other at the beginning of the 20th century.

The Victoria Theatre was originally built as Singapore's Town Hall. Designed by John Bennett, its construction took place between 1856 and 1862. It was one of the first Singapore buildings to reflect the Italian Renaissance style that represented the beginning of Victorian Revivalism. The Town Hall had a dual function as a theatre performance venue as well as for office and meeting uses. However, demand for the use of the theatre saw it being fully utilised as a performance venue, resulting in the Town Hall offices moving out in 1883.

In 1903, the Victoria Concert Hall was built, originally as a memorial to Queen Victoria who had passed away in 1901. It was designed by Regent Alfred John Bidwell of Swan & MacLaren.

Today, we see the statue of Sir Stamford Raffles standing in front of the Victoria Memorial Hall. The Raffles statue was first located at the Esplanade, and officially unveiled on Jubilee Day, 27 June 1887, by Governor of the Straits Settlements Sir Frederick Weld. The eight-feet-tall bronze statue represented Raffles in deep thought with his head bent and arms folded. In addition to Raffles' coat of arms, the base of the pedestal had a map of the Malacca Straits and the geographical land mass that formed British Malaya.

The Raffles statue remained in this spot until 1919, when Singapore celebrated the centenary of its founding. As part of the centenary plans, the government decided that the statue should be restored and re-installed at a position befitting for Raffles. Furthermore, the relocation was prompted by reclamation works on the Esplanade.

The relocation of the Raffles statue was overseen by a sub-committee of the Centenary Committee. Following its move to the new site in front of the Victoria Memorial Hall, the setting of the statue was improved with the addition of a semi-circular Italian colonnade. A commemorative plaque of the centenary of Singapore's founding was added on the plinth of the statue. At the rear side of the pedestal is another small tablet that documents the statue's relocation to the Victoria Memorial Hall site. This relocated statue was unveiled by Governor of the Straits Settlements Sir Arthur Young on 6 February 1919.

The relocation was received with public approval. An article in the *Straits Times* reported on the event and commented that "the statue is no longer subjected to the indignity of being struck by footballs, nor of the base being used either as seat of vantage by enthusiastic admirers of the game. Sir Stamford no longer turns his back on the church but gazes at the spot where he first landed, the mouth of the Singapore River."

Following the Japanese invasion of the Malay Peninsula and Singapore in February 1942, the Japanese military administrators of Syonan ordered the Raffles statue to be dismantled. The statue's removal signalled Japanese victory and the end of British rule. It was stored at the Raffles Museum for the duration of the Japanese Occupation. After the war, the statue was reinstated at the Victoria Memorial Hall site by Governor of Singapore Sir Franklin Gimson on 6 July 1946, the anniversary of Sir Stamford Raffles 165th birthday. However, its Italian colonnade was not reinstalled.

Victoria Theatre
& Concert Hall

9 Empress Place
S(179556)

GOODWOOD PARK HOTEL

A prominent landmark of Scotts Road for over a century, this castle-like building was constructed in 1900 as the Teutonia Club, a gathering place for the German-speaking community residing in Singapore. The original tower structure was designed by famed architect Regent Albert John Bidwell of Swan & MacLaren, and constructed at a cost of $20,000.

With the outbreak of World War I in August 1914, Germany and Britain became enemies. German nationals in Singapore were detained and their properties confiscated as enemy properties by the Custodian of Enemy Property. After the end of World War I, the colonial government sold the Teutonia Club building to the Manasseh brothers (Morris, Ezekiel and Ellis). Renamed as Goodwood Hall, it went through various uses, including a public concert hall, dance hall and restaurant. In 1929, it was renamed Goodwood Park Hotel upon its conversion into a hotel.

The hotel was requisitioned for use as a residence for Japanese army officers during the Japanese Occupation of Singapore. However after World War II, the building was used by the British army's War Crimes Investigation Teams to probe the war crimes of the Japanese. The hotel was also the venue for a war crimes court to prosecute minor Japanese war criminals.

In September 1947, the hotel reverted to civilian ownership, and its doors were re-opened. Under the management of Vivian Bath, stepson of Ezekiel Manasseh, the hotel became popular with tourists in the 1950s and 1960s. This period further witnessed the physical expansion of the hotel to take on the character that we see today. The expansions included a new wing to the Tower Block in 1956, and additions of the Parklane Wing and the Mayfair Wing in 1968 and 1970 respectively.

Over the years, many highly-esteemed personalities have stayed at this hotel during their visits to Singapore, including the Prince of Wales, the Duke of Richmond, King Baudoin of Belgium and Sir Noel Coward. In 1968, the hotel was acquired by Singapore tycoon Khoo Teck Puat, and it has been restored and repaired on several occasions since 1977. The Tower Block of Goodwood Park Hotel was gazetted as a National Monument of Singapore in 1989.

Goodwood Park Hotel

22 Scotts Road
S(228221)

HOUSE OF TAN YOKE NEE

Along the junction of Penang Road and Clemenceau Avenue is a Southern Chinese-style house sited on a small, high-ground slope set back from the road. Built in 1885 as the residence of Tan Yoke Nee, this house was intended to reflect his status as a successful Chinese gentleman. What motivated him to build his house in 1885, diagonally across the Government House (official residence of the Governor constructed in 1869) is a mystery lost to history. However, Tan spared no expenses in demonstrating his wealth and social position as he imported building materials and hired craftsmen from China to realise his mansion. He resided in this house for a few years before returning to his hometown in Chaozhou, where he built a larger mansion as his permanent retirement home.

House of
Tan Yoke Nee

101 Penang Road
S(238466)

Ownership of the house shifted from the Tan family to the Straits Settlements Government when it was acquired to serve as the official residence of the Singapore Railway Master at the turn of the 20th century. The Singapore Railway service's main station was then located at Tank Road. In 1912, the house became the St Mary's Home and School for Girls, managed by the Anglican Church of Singapore. In 1938, the house was taken over by the Salvation Army and was used as its local headquarters for the next five decades, before it was sold to the Cockpit Hotel Group in 1991.

The house was subsequently acquired by the Wing Tai Group, and its new lease of life began with a full restoration according to traditional Chaozhou building methods, and adaptive re-use as the Asian campus for the University of Chicago School of Business.

The House of Tan Yoke Nee was gazetted as a National Monument in 1973.

Architectural Features

Exhibiting superb Chaozhou courtyard house architecture, this residential house has a "four points of gold" (*si dian jin*) planning layout. It has a recessed entrance hallway and four double-pitched gable ends. The garbled roof of the house is shaped according to the five elements of Metal, Wood, Water, Fire, and Earth. The roof ridges are decorated with lovely handcrafted porcelain shard works known as *qian ci*, which are fabricated via a cut-and-paste technique known as *jian nian*. These depict flora, animals, birds, fish and human figurines in bas relief. The roofs have spirals on all the front hips.

TAN YOKE NEE (1827–1902)

According to Song Ong Siang's account in *One Hundred Years' History of the Chinese in Singapore*, Tan Yoke Nee started out as a Teochew cloth merchant who gained the friendship of Sultan Abu Bakar and his family while they were still residing in Singapore.

Tan was a rugged pioneer who later carved pepper and gambier plantations out of the jungles of Johor. By 1866, he had become a successful pepper and gambier trader, owning several lots of land in Johor Bahru's town centre. He was also one of the most prominent revenue farmers in Johor, having plantations, spirit and opium farms within the *kangchu* system. He further started a market, and possessed many properties and shophouses.

Tan held great political influence and fiscal powers in Johor. Trusted by Sultan Abu Bakar, he was appointed Major-China of Johor in 1870 to maintain law and order within the Chinese community, and to act as an intermediary between the Malay and British authorities. In the history of Malaysia, he is the only Chinese to be ever appointed this rank in the Kapitan system. Within Johor, Tan was also the head of the Ngee Heng Kongsi (a Teochew offshoot of the *Tiandihui*), a quasi-military revolutionary brotherhood.

In 1885, Tan moved back to Singapore upon his retirement as Major-China of Johor. For some years he lived at his mansion at Clemenceau Avenue before retiring in his native Chaozhou in Guangdong Province, China. He continues to have a road named after him within the town of Johor Bahru—Jalan Tan Hiok Nee.

ISTANA & SRI TEMASEK

During the colonial period, the Istana—then known as the Government House—and Sri Temasek were the official residences of the British Governor and the Colonial Secretary respectively. This was the second Government House in Singapore. (The first was constructed at Bukit Larangan shortly after Sir Stamford Raffles arrived in Singapore in 1819, but demolished four decades later to make way for Fort Canning.)

In 1867, Governor Sir Harry Ord, who found the temporary accommodations provided at Leonie Hill Hall to be inadequate, instructed that a new Government House be built. The colonial administration acquired 106 acres of land from the nutmeg estate of Charles Robert Prinsep for its construction.

The Governor's official residence was designed by Major J.F.A. McNair, Chief Engineer of the Public Works Department. Inspired by the architecture of the Italian Renaissance, he planned a building in the shape of a cross, and external façades featuring Ionic influences with Corinthian pillars and pilasters to the towers. Holding a concurrent appointment as Superintendent of Convicts, McNair employed Indian convicts to build the property. The foundation stone was laid in July 1867, and the house was completed within two years. Construction of the residence of the Colonial Secretary commenced thereafter. The first guest to stay at Government House was the Duke of Edinburgh, who arrived in Singapore in December 1869.

The Government House was sited in a former nutmeg plantation with mature fruit-tree orchards. Its landscaping was designed by William Kent, who opted for a style that focused on nature as a garden. As a result, the character of the 1830 plantation was retained within the landscape of Government House. With the passage of time,

new additions were made to the grounds. These included the laying of a nine-hole golf course during Sir Arthur Young's governorship between 1911 and 1919.

Following Singapore's attainment of self-government in 1959, the Government House was renamed Istana Negara Singapura, while the former Colonial Secretary's residence became Sri Temasek. The Istana and Sri Temasek have been the official residences of Singapore's President and Prime Minister respectively since.

From 1869 till present, the Istana has been the official residence of 21 British Governors, two *Yang Di-Pertuan Negara* (Heads of State) and six Presidents of Singapore. It continues to be the venue for state and ceremonial events. The grounds of the Istana are open to the public on selected public holidays, such as New Year's Day and Chinese New Year.

Both the Istana and Sri Temasek are gazetted National Monuments of Singapore, and have been restored over the years. Sri Temasek's recent restoration won the 2008 URA Architectural Heritage Award (Category A).

Istana &
Sri Temasek
Orchard Road
S(238823)

MACDONALD HOUSE

Located across the Dhoby Ghaut MRT station alongside a row of pre-war conserved shophouses is the MacDonald House. This multi-storey structure was constructed in 1949 for the Hong Kong and Shanghai Banking Corporation (HSBC). It was the first large office building to be erected in the post-World War II period, and was designed by the architectural firm of Palmer & Turner. For many years it housed a branch of the HSBC, as well as many international firms, mainly British, American and Australian.

Named after Mr Malcolm MacDonald, this 60-year-old red brick building has a reinforced concrete framed structure and is Neo-Georgian in character. It is likely to be the only office building clad in facing brick left in this district.

Located above the entrance of the bank is an interesting bas relief panel that reflects the historical heritage of the HSBC. The British royal coat of arms is prominently positioned above a depiction of two Chinese traders (in pigtails and long gown garment of the Qing Dynasty) overseeing a Chinese coolie loading goods at a harbour. A Chinese junk and a western cargo ship are in the harbour. This panel highlights the role played by the bank in facilitating international commerce between the East and West.

MacDonald House
40A Orchard Road
S(238837)

The MacDonald House is a symbolic reminder of the Indonesian Confrontation, one of the key historical events that had affected political developments in Singapore and the region. On 10 May 1965, the building was bombed by terrorists as a mark of Indonesia's stand against the formation of the Federation of Malaysia. This bombing is among the most severe terrorist attacks in Singapore's history, and highlights the country's vulnerability to terrorism.

A Singapore National Monument, the MacDonald House has been restored, and continues to function as a commercial building, occupied by a branch of an American bank together with offices of Singapore firms and foreign multi-national corporations.

MAGHAIN ABOTH SYNAGOGUE & CHESED-EL SYNAGOGUE

The Jewish have been residing in Singapore for over 180 years. Ever since the 1830 Singapore census documented the local residency of nine Shephardic Jews from Baghdad, the Jewish community has been an important component of Singapore's social fabric.

In 1841, the community constructed their first synagogue on a piece of leased land along South Bridge Road. The synagogue functioned here until Sir Manasseh Meyer, a highly successful Jewish entrepreneur, oversaw its relocation to new premises at Waterloo Street in 1878 with the construction of the Maghain Aboth Synagogue. The memory of the old synagogue is preserved with the street name of Synagogue Street.

Maghain Aboth Synagogue

Construction of the Maghain Aboth (which means 'Shield of Our Fathers' in Hebrew) Synagogue began in 1871, and it was consecrated on 4 April 1878. Originally a single-storey building, it was subsequently expanded with the addition of a second-

storey balcony. Facing Waterloo Street, the building possesses the façade of a 19th-century bungalow, and street pedestrians will see a magnificent house with a covered carriage porch entrance. The Star of David is prominently displayed on the façade.

The synagogue comprises a main prayer hall in which the men worship at the ground floor, and women worship from the second-storey balcony. Men enter the synagogue through the main entrance, while women use a separate side entrance for access to the balcony.

Within the synagogue is the Ark. Placed on a raised platform, the Ark is oriented westward towards the direction of Jerusalem. It is covered with the parochet (an embroidered curtain), and the Torah is kept in a niche within the Ark.

Maghain Aboth Synagogue is the venue of Jewish religious festivals and community life. Births, deaths, marriages and many other social events are observed here. The building has been restored in recent years, and a new addition to the compound is the seven-storey Jacob Ballas Centre.

Maghain Aboth Synagogue
24 Waterloo Street
S(187950)

Chesed-El Synagogue

Located at Oxley Rise, the Chesed-El Synagogue (which means 'Bounty of God' in Hebrew) was constructed in 1905 by Sir Manasseh Meyer.

Singapore's Jewish populace had expanded from 300 in 1871 to 1,200 by 1900. This Jewish community comprised Ashkenazi Jews (European Jews) and Shephardic Jews, and more religious services were required. To relieve the overcrowding at the Maghain Aboth Synagogue, Sir Meyer provided the land and footed the bill to construct a private synagogue next to his home, Belle Vue, at Oxley Rise.

Designed by Regent Alfred John Bidwell from the architectural firm of Swan & MacLaren, this three-storey building is constructed in the late Renaissance style. Facing Oxley Rise, the synagogue's entrance features a projected covered carriage porch.

The side elevations of the building consist of flat-sided pillars resting on rectangular bases, aligned with the second-storey pilasters that curve out into arched double-leafed windows with round and half mooned fanlights. The synagogue's interior is constructed as a big hall with fluted columns intersected with two sets of moulding. Their square moulded capitals are joined with arches at the top of the ceiling. Meyer's initial 'M' can be clearly seen within the decorative moulding.

Similar to the Maghain Aboth Synagogue, this synagogue has a main prayer hall where men worship at the ground floor and women worship from the second-storey gallery sited above the carriage porch. Men enter the synagogue through the main entrance while women use another ground floor entrance to access to the gallery.

The Torah is kept within the Ark placed on a raised wooden platform. Sited in front of the congregation, the scrolls of the Torah are retrieved and read every Sabbath by selected male members of the community.

Religious services are held regularly alternating between the Maghain Aboth and Chesed-El Synagogues. The former is owned by the trustees of the Jewish Synagogue Ordinance and managed by the Jewish Welfare Board, while the Sir Manasseh Meyer Trust owns and manages the latter. Both synagogues were gazetted as National Monuments in 1998.

Chesed-El
Synagogue

2 Oxley Rise
S(238693)

NATIONAL MUSEUM OF SINGAPORE

The National Museum is the first purpose-built museum in Singapore. Consisting of a central dome with two parallel rectangular blocks to its right and left, the building was designed in the Neo-Palladian and Renaissance style by architects Henry McCallum and Major J.F.A. McNair.

This building was constructed in 1882 as the Raffles Library and Museum, and was officially opened on 12 October 1887. It was internationally known for its zoological and ethnographic collection of Southeast Asia (specialising in Malaya and British Borneo).

In 1960, the Raffles Library separated from the Museum, with the Museum's focus shifting towards Singapore's history and aligning with the nation-building efforts of the country. Renamed the National Museum, this restructuring witnessed the break-up of its magnificent zoological collection. A large segment was transferred to the University of Singapore's Department of Biology (which is now the Raffles Museum of Biodiversity Research, Department of Biological Sciences in the National University of Singapore), while others were donated to museums in India and Malaysia.

The National Museum was gazetted as a National Monument in 1992. It came under the National Heritage Board in 1993, and had its name changed to the Singapore History Museum. Closed for a $136-million restoration and additions project between 2003 and 2006, the museum was re-launched as the National Museum of Singapore on 7 December 2006 by President S.R. Nathan.

The museum was expanded with a new extension wing at the rear. While marking the addition to the museum, the glass structure at the concourse provides visitors with opportunities to appreciate the architectural heritage of the old museum, such as its dome's zinc fish-scale tiles and stained glass panels.

These 2006 additions added over 2,800 sqm of gallery space to the museum. The key new additions include a glass rotunda for the exhibition of Singapore's history, a 250-seat underground auditorium, and new cafes and restaurants.

National
Museum of
Singapore

93 Stamford Road,
S(178897)

ORCHARD ROAD PRESBYTERIAN CHURCH

The Orchard Road Presbyterian Church was the first Presbyterian Church to be constructed in Singapore, and is located at the junction of Orchard Road and Bras Basah Road. Founded in 1856 to administer to the Scottish business community in Singapore, this landmark is also popularly referred to as the Greja Kechil ('small church' in vernacular Malay) and the Scotch Church, in reference to the original congregation of Scots.

The land on which the church stands was granted by the Governor of Singapore in 1875, following an application by Reverend William Dale. The foundation stone for the first church building on the present site was laid by Colonel Anson on 1 August 1877, and construction of the church was completed in 1878.

This is one of the few remaining buildings constructed in the 19th century to be found in Singapore. The one-storey religious structure has tiled pitch roofs built in the Palladian style, with repetitive wall openings at regular intervals along the side elevations. A tower and entrance portico facing Orchard Road accentuates the front of the building. A cupola supported by slender columns sits on top of the tower with finials at four corners.

During the post-World War II years, the church witnessed expansion within its compound. A Sunday School and servants' quarters were added in 1953, and an extension to the Church Hall was completed in 1954. The sanctuary was extended in 1975, and 1985 saw the church being further expanded with the construction of Dunman Hall. The Tomlinson Hall, added as a side extension in 1921, was demolished in 2002.

This church retains a sense of place and the social history of early colonial Singapore within Bras Basah, despite the unsightly erection of an Electronic Road Pricing (ERP) gantry in front of its lawn.

While the original congregation was Scottish, Orchard Road Presbyterian Church has reached out to other peoples, and it now has English, Mandarin, Indonesian and German-speaking sections in its congregation.

Orchard Road
Presbyterian
Church

3 Orchard Road
S(238825)

PRINSEP STREET PRESBYTERIAN CHURCH

The Prinsep Street Presbyterian Church is one of the most significant buildings located along Prinsep Street. This structure was first known as the Malay Chapel, and was used as a Malay boys' school by Reverend Benjamin Peach Keaberry of the London Missionary Society in 1843. It was renamed the Prinsep Street Church in 1885 following its acquisition by the Presbyterian Church. In the succeeding years, the church housed congregations of the Straits Chinese and Teochew Chinese, as well as the Sophia Cooke Chinese Girls School.

The church is also well known within the local Boys' Brigade (BB) community as the birthplace of the Singapore Boys' Brigade movement in 1930. James Milner Fraser, a former member of 23rd Aberdeen Company and 23rd London Company, founded the 1st Singapore Company at Prinsep Street Church after moving to Singapore for work as an architect. Assisted by Quek Eng Moh and Dong Chui Sing, the company began its activities in youth work. Within a few years, Fraser of Singapore (as he became known within BB circles) had set up BB companies in various churches, including Kampong Kapor Methodist Church, Geylang Chinese Methodist Church, Paya Lebar Methodist Church as well as school-sponsored companies in Anglo-Chinese School and St Andrew's School.

The current church building was constructed in 1930 on the site of the former church, which was demolished. The foundation stone was laid by Mr Song Ong Siang on 5 March 1930, and the new church was officially opened on 4 February 1931. Displaying Romanesque-style architecture with the use of red bricks, a notable feature of its façade is the raised brickwork on the tower and belfry. The church became Prinsep Street Presbyterian Church in November 1931 when it formally joined the Synod of the English Presbytery.

Prinsep Street Presbyterian Church is a National Monument and a marked Historic Site for being the birthplace of the Singapore Boys' Brigade Movement.

Prinsep Street
Presbyterian
Church

77 Prinsep Street
S(188649)

PRINSEP STREET
PRESBYTERIAN CHURCH

The Boys' Brigade in Singapore

Singapore's first company of the Boys' Brigade was formed on 12 January 1930 at Prinsep Street Presbyterian Church by James Milner Fraser. This was soon followed by the formation of more companies in other Christian churches. In 1936, there were six Boys' Brigade companies in Singapore, and the Singapore Battalion was formed. By January 2000, the Boys' Brigade had 70 companies with about 5000 members island-wide and is one of the oldest uniformed groups in Singapore. Its aims are the advancement of Christ's Kingdom among Boys and the promotion of habits of Obedience, Reverence, Discipline, Self-Respect and all that tend towards a true Christian Manliness. The members of the Boys' Brigade hold regular meetings and activities that include drills, physical training, bible classes and games.

NATIONAL HERITAGE BOARD

ST GEORGE'S CHURCH

The next time you travel in the Tanglin area along Napier Road, do keep a lookout for a charming little church located next to the golf course at Minden Road, across the Singapore Botanic Gardens. St George's Church is one of Singapore's national monuments, donning simple architecture that is functional and lovely to look at.

During Singapore's early days as a Straits Settlement, the British established an army garrison in Tanglin. Tanglin Barracks, as it became known, provided a permanent presence for British troops to be stationed to protect British economic and strategic military interests in Malaya, as well as to protect the sea routes from Britain to Australia and China.

A garrison (or military) church was set up to serve the religious needs of officers and men of the garrison. But as the military presence grew in Singapore, it was obvious that a larger church was needed, and hence a new building was constructed at Minden Road.

This new church, known as St George's Church, was designed by Captain William Henry Stanbury of the Royal Engineers, and built between 1910 and 1913 on the site of a nutmeg plantation. It was an Anglican Church even though it was then not within the jurisdiction of the Anglican Diocese of Singapore. This was due to the religious background of the soldiers who were mostly Anglicans from the Church of England. The first pastors were military chaplains and they ministered the gospel to the soldiers as well as to the civilian population in the area. Hence, the church had both a military and civilian congregation.

During the Japanese Occupation, the church was converted into an ammunition store. After the war, the church was rededicated as a garrison church and refurbished. It continued to serve military servicemen, their families and the community at large.

The British military began its withdrawal from the Far East in 1968, including Singapore. In 1971, the withdrawal was complete, and the church was transferred to the jurisdiction of the Anglican Diocese of Singapore. This began its new phase of life as a civilian church.

In 1978, St George's Church was gazetted as a National Monument.

St George's
Church

Minden Road
S(248816)

Architectural Features

St George's Church was built in the Basilica style, and constructed entirely of brick. It is basically a long, rectangular barn with columns all around it. Following the Greek form of a temple, it has a pitched roof with the triangular gables and columns in the arches down each side and on each end.

The brickwork and construction of the church has some interesting features, such as "egg-and-a-dart" mouldings, where the bricks have a row of eggs and little arrow heads (also known as darts) used to decorate the interior; and "teeth" mouldings, where the different manner of laying the bricks provide an impression of it as a row of teeth.

Keen-eyed visitors will notice various types of arches in the church. There are circular and double arches with one on top of the other. These arches help to support each other, providing the building with structural stability, and preventing the roof from crashing down. In addition, you can find segment arches (a segment of a circle that forms a flatter arch). It is a result of having two bricks resting against each other.

The roof is constructed from timber, and has thin steel ties that support the entire structure and holds everything in place. This structure is known as a truss. The trusses sit in tiny stone brackets (called corbels) built into the brickwork between the arches.

If you visit this church, you will also notice that the architecture allows plenty of natural light to filter into the building, as well as the unrestricted movement of breeze to flow through it. This is important in a tropical environment.

THE LICH GATE

At the entrance of the church is the Lich Gate which dates back to World War II. Allied soldiers and prisoners-of-war (POW) were imprisoned in Changi Prison and surrounding area. POWs died while in captivity and were buried on the grounds of Purdy Camp—a Boy Scout campsite located outside the prison.

The Lich Gate was built in December 1942 by the British 18th Division to beautify the entrance to the POW cemetery. Major Harper, R.E., who designed the cemetery, may also have designed the Lich Gate. When the cemetery was closed in October 1944, 41 British officers had been buried alongside eight Dutch officers, 472 British soldiers, 58 Dutch soldiers, one British nurse and one Dutch civilian.

After the war, the graves were exhumed and relocated for re-burial in Kranji Commonwealth War Cemetery. The Lich Gate was salvaged in 1952 and brought to St George's Garrison Church, where it was dedicated on 14 December 1952.

With the withdrawal of the British military in 1971, the Lich Gate was dismantled and brought to the United Kingdom by the British. It was re-assembled at the Queen's Division Depot, Bassingbourne Barracks in Hertfordshire. In 1978, a replica of the Lich Gate was constructed as part of the church's restoration work.

SINGAPORE BOTANIC GARDENS

Located just a few kilometres from the city centre, the Botanic Gardens offers scenic views and respite from the polluted city air.

Apart from its historical value, having been founded in 1859, the Botanic Gardens has a special place as a lifelong companion in the hearts of those in their twilight years. Tradition is not about to be broken, for their grandchildren are now enjoying the beautiful flowers and fascinating creatures the Gardens offers. Few other places allow quiet contemplation amidst the wonders of the natural world without admission fees or physical exertion. This places the Botanic Gardens one echelon above other tourist attractions.

For all its nostalgic atmosphere, the Botanic Gardens is no slouch in its chief purpose as a centre for botanical research. Since the heyday of rubber cultivation in which it played a critical role, the Gardens did not let up in its efforts to generate and propagate botanical knowledge. For example, the laboratories running orchid hybridisation and breeding experiments initiated in the early 20th century are still in operation, but now upgraded with state-of-the-art equipment. Their results can be admired in the National Orchid Garden. The Singapore Herbarium, a powerhouse of taxonomic research and an internationally important repository of priceless reference specimens from Southeast Asia and around the world, also calls the Gardens its home.

Where there are plants making food through photosynthesis, there are animals as well. While it is unrealistic to expect orang utans and gibbons to swing through the trees as they do in vast tracts of primeval forest in Borneo, patient and observant visitors may be rewarded with almost equally spectacular sights. One of the most iconic of these is a flock of endangered Whistling Ducks that, by virtue of their bulk, resemble World War II bombers in flight. Landing astonishingly close to people, they waddle in a fashion that captivates children and adults alike.

Circling the serene lakeside, one may also chance upon a White-breasted Waterhen scurrying across one's path with a delicious morsel in its bill, admire the resplendent and acrobatic Bee-eaters dive in and take off in a splash of glittering droplets, fear for the life of a juvenile Yellow Bittern teetering on the flimsy shoots of water plants, or be awed by the enormous Purple Heron as it lands majestically yet somewhat comically on a tree. If one is really lucky, one may even see rare Red-legged Crakes mating on the driveway at the Visitor Centre!

In recent years, there have been public proposals to the Government for the Singapore Botanical Gardens to be nominated for listing as a UNESCO World Natural Heritage Site, joining the international ranks of the Botanical Garden of Padua and Kew Gardens of London.

Singapore
Botanic Gardens

1 Cluny Road
S(259569)

THANDAYUTHAPANI TEMPLE (CHETTIAR'S TEMPLE)

Popularly known as the Tank Road Temple, this Hindu temple was founded by Chettiar immigrants during the 19th century. Dedicated to the deity Thandayuthapani, the temple was first constructed during 1859 by the Nattukottai Chettiars. The Chettiars were traditional money-lenders in the early Singapore society. They established an alternative informal money market to that of the established merchant banks that did not provide small loans to individuals without collateral. Peoples of all ethnicities thus tapped on the services of the Chettiars.

The entrance tower (*gopuram*) is a very important feature of this Southern Indian Hindu temple. The present five-tier *gopuram* was consecrated in 1983 and it is dedicated to the Lord Murugan.

The figurines on the *gopuram*, arches, columns and prayer halls were restored and repaired during the periodic renovations in line with Hindu religious practices to re-consecrate the temple.

This temple is well known in Singapore for the annual culmination of the Thaipusam festival. Prior to participating in Thaipusam, devotees prepare themselves by undergoing fasting and abstinence. Devotees of Murugan carrying *kavadis* (skewers that pierce their cheeks or bodies) commence their journey on foot from the Vishnu Temple at Serangoon Road and conclude their walk at Thandayuthapani Temple. To be removed only at Thandayuthapani Temple, the devotees carry their *kavadis* as a test of their religious faith. During this festival, the roads through which the devotees would walk from Serangoon Road towards Tank Road would be cordoned off for their exclusive use. The temple is also a popular wedding venue for Hindus, with many holding their celebrations in the wedding hall.

Thandayuthapani Temple

15 Tank Road
S(238065)

WEST

BABA HOUSE

Not to be mistaken with the Peranakan (Baba) Museum at Armenian Street, Baba House is a restored three-storey Straits Chinese residential house located in the historic district of Blair Plain. Constructed during the 1860s, it was the home of Wee Bin, a Chinese shipping tycoon.

Baba House was purchased and donated to the National University of Singapore (NUS) by Ms Agnes Tan in honour of her late father, Tun Tan Cheng Lock (1883–1960). Tun Tan was a Malacca-born Straits Chinese entrepreneur, founder of the Malayan Chinese Association (MCA), a community leader and Finance Minister in Tunku Abdul Rahman's cabinet. Ms Tan's gift was made with the intent to preserve Straits Chinese culture, and to educate the younger generations about the history, traditions and architecture of the Peranakan people.

Staff and students of the NUS Architecture Department and the Department of Southeast Asian Studies were involved in the house's restoration process, working together with the Urban Redevelopment Authority (URA) Conservation Section. An archaeological dig was also commissioned to reveal insights of domestic life within this 19th-century house.

Restoration work involved repairs to both the exterior façade and the interior space of the building. Elaborate and intricately carved wooden windows, doors and partition screens in the interior were retained and restored in accordance with the original character of this Peranakan house.

Baba House
157 Neil Road
S(088883)

The first two storeys of Baba House are managed by NUS Museum, and used as an exhibition space to showcase Peranakan social history and heritage. Amongst its key exhibits is the Peranakan bridal chamber, which sheds light on the traditional customs and rites involved in a Peranakan wedding. The top floor is an exhibition gallery for use by artists to display their works in interpreting Peranakan culture. The Peranakan Association of Singapore also has its offices here.

Due to the fragile nature of the house, visits are limited to small groups of 12. Prior appointments are required for all visits.

CHURCH OF ST TERESA

Within the district of Bukit Purmei is the Church of St Teresa. The land on which the church stands belonged to the estate of Sultan Abu Bakar of Johor, and was purchased by French missionaries for this purpose. Named after St Teresa of the Child Jesus, the patron saint of the missions, this Roman Catholic church was built by Father Emile Mariette and Father Stephen Lee from 1926 to 1929 for the use of Hokkien Catholics who settled in a new Chinese village that eventually became Kampong Bahru.

The Church of St Teresa is a monument that symbolises the contributions of French missionaries and Singapore Catholics to the country's development and the local community in the 20th century. Beginning in 1929, St Teresa Convent was founded on church premises as a girls' school for the daughters of Indian port workers at Pasir Panjang wharves.

In 1938, the church founded St Teresa High School to provide Chinese vernacular education for Chinese children within the neighbourhood. During the Japanese Occupation, the school served as a refugee centre. After the war, St Teresa High School became a school-cum-orphanage with the founding of St Teresa's Orphanage. During this period, the church further founded the De La Salle School and Sacred Hearts Boys School within its premises. The church also contributed to the construction of the Carmelite Convent, Aljunied Canossian Convent (Orphanage) and the Catholic High School.

Architectural Features

Located on a hill at Kampong Bahru Road, the Church of St Teresa is the only church in Singapore with a dome on the face and two smaller domes on either side of the building. The architectural style reflects that of the Neo-Byzantine (Byzantine Gothic), which is rarely seen here.

The designer, Emile Brizay, is believed to have been inspired by the 19th-century Eglise Sacre Coeur Montmartre in Paris, though others have commented that it is an exact duplicate.

FORMER NANYANG UNIVERSITY
(NANYANG TECHNOLOGICAL UNIVERSITY)

Located at the western corner of Singapore in Jurong, Nanyang University (South Seas University in vernacular Chinese) was the first Chinese-language university to be founded in Southeast Asia. It was established in Singapore in 1953, and was incorporated as a company. Its founding was realised through the efforts of the Singapore Hokkien Huay Kuan and Mr Tan Lark Sye, who donated land for it. This university was also constructed with financial contributions from Chinese people of all walks of life across the region; they included wealthy merchants and humble coolies. In the 1950s, Nanyang University was an important symbol of the spirit of the Overseas Chinese community and its selfless commitment towards advancing Chinese-medium tertiary education in Singapore and Malaya.

This university later merged with the University of Singapore in 1980 to form the National University of Singapore. The campus was known as Nanyang Technological Institute in 1981. A decade later, it became the Nanyang Technological University. The structures were gazetted as National Monuments of Singapore in 1998.

The original buildings and structures of Nanyang University are the Library and Administration Building, University Arch (Nantah Arch) and University Memorial. They carry Chinese "National Style" architectural features as employed by their architect Ng Keng Siang. In such a style, the built structures were constructed out of reinforced concrete while adopting the scale and form of modern buildings, but with the retention of a Chinese roof and its associated ornamentation.

Library and Administration Building

Part of the original campus at 12 Nanyang Drive, the library building was constructed at a cost of half a million dollars, funded by the donations of Penang businessman Lim Lean Teng. It later became the administration building of Nanyang University. Nanyang University began the formal commencement of classes at this building on 15 March 1956.

Nantah Arch

Situated at Yunnan Garden, the Nantah Arch served as the gateway to the university for 25 years. Constructed in the style of traditional Chinese "*pai fang*", the arch features the Chinese characters "*Nanyang Daxue*" in the calligraphy of Master Yu You Ren. It was officially presented to the public in 1955. However, due to the development of housing and roads in this area, the Nantah Arch was separated from the campus. The surrounding ground is now a public park.

Nanyang University Memorial

The Nanyang University Memorial at 42 Nanyang Avenue was unveiled on 30 March 1958 to mark the completion of the first phase of the Nanyang University building programme.

Former Nanyang University

Nanyang Avenue, Nanyang Drive

KEPPEL RAILWAY STATION

At the turn of the 20th century, Singapore operated a railway service within the island. The main train station was based at Tank Road (near to present-day Church of the Sacred Heart) and a regular train service ran daily, plying a network of stations along the urban town comprising Orchard Road, Cuppage Road, Newton Circus and Bukit Timah Road, as well as the rural stations located within the plantations cultivating pineapples, pepper and gambier at Bukit Panjang, Kranji and Woodlands.

In 1923, the opening of the Causeway connecting Singapore to the Johor state resulted in Singapore having a direct railway link with the Malay Peninsula. The Straits Settlements Government then sold the existing Singapore railway line to Malaya Railway for 4.136 million Straits Settlements dollars. The Singapore line was re-routed to commence from Tanjong Pagar to Bukit Merah, and to traverse on a western direction, linking up with the original Bukit Timah Road segment of line towards Woodlands and Johor Bahru. The original rail line linking Tank Road towards Newton Circus and part of Bukit Timah Road was scrapped.

The main station along this re-routed line was to be based at Keppel Road in Tanjong Pagar, a stone's throw away from the Keppel Harbour. It was built on reclaimed land between 1929 and 1932 as the Keppel Railway Station, and became the most magnificent railway station along the entire Malayan Railway line. Sir Cecil Clementi Smith, Governor of the Straits Settlements, officially opened this station in 1932.

Architectural Features

The Keppel Railway Station was designed by DS Petrovitch of the architectural firm Swan & MacLaren. A graduate of the Architectural Association School of Architecture in London, this Serbian architect's work has withstood the test of time, with the station having been in continuous use for over 75 years.

Petrovitch's Classical design of Keppel Railway Station is said to be inspired by the Helsinki Station, designed by Eliel Saarinen. The station's front entrance elevation is characterised by three main arches and two side arches. The wall is decorated with four sculptures depicting Commerce, Agriculture, Industry and Transport. These are the work of Italian sculptor Cavalieri Rudolfo Nolli.

Keppel Railway Station

30 Keppel Road, S(089059)

LABRADOR NATURE RESERVE

In the midst of a sprawling metropolis of fume-belching cars and ships, there is refuge to be found. Sandwiched between two container terminals at one of the busiest ports in the world is an improbable enclave—an ancient enclave of nature holding out amidst the industrial arsenal of man. Cramped within a mere 10 hectares is a motley mix of forest, sea-cliff vegetation, rocky shore and coral communities that awaken to the foghorns of intercontinental shipping every morning. When one walks through this forest of benevolent trees, the canopy creates a dark and tranquil sanctuary beneath the scorching equatorial sun, and one can only feel gratitude for the rejuvenating fresh air and melodious bird song that nature gives for free.

One of Labrador's most illustrious former residents, for whom the Nature Reserves Ordinance was enacted here in 1951, was the *Dipteris conjugata*. This Triassic fern has been on earth eight times longer than mankind.

Beneath the waves that caress the foot of the cliff, life flourishes. The lilting tentacles of coral polyps, pulsating bells of translucent jellyfish, sinuous undulations of finned muscles and a myriad of other manifestations of nature's bizarre designs conjure an underwater scene not unlike the prehistoric seas which existed long before any creature could breathe atmospheric oxygen.

Academics may criticise the diminutive area of Labrador Nature Reserve in relation to the national parks of larger countries, and argue ad infinitum on the isolation of gene pools by ecological deserts (read concrete jungle), but this diminutive hiding place for native biodiversity is a jewel in a city-state where a respectable Gross Domestic Product coexists with nature in very nearly the best way possible.

Fort Pasir Panjang

An old British military fort is located within the Labrador Nature Reserve. This is the Fort Pasir Panjang, which was constructed in 1886 as one of the series of coastal artillery forts to protect Keppel Harbour. The fort was expanded in the 1930s with addition of two six-inch, 16-tonne guns pointed seawards in anticipation of a southern seaborne invasion. However, the 1942 invasion of Singapore saw Japanese forces advancing from the northern Johor Straits instead.

Contrary to popular belief, the turrets of these coastal guns could be turned in various directions. During the Battle for Pasir Panjang, these guns saw action against the advancing Japanese troops. In the post-war period, the fort was decommissioned and closed down.

Supporting the gunnery was a complex of bunkers and tunnels, some of which, having been ensconced in the verdant cradle of tropical flora like a miniature Angkor Wat, became lost. In 2001, two tunnels were rediscovered under the old fort. These structures were most likely used as an ammunition storage facility and shelter for the soldiers.

Daily guided tours to these tunnels are conducted daily.

Labrador Nature Reserve
Labrador Villa Road

PALMER ROAD

Tanjong Pagar, where Palmer Road is located, is an important district within the history of Singapore. Known as Tanjong Malang during the 18th century, this coastal area as made up of fishing villages occupied by the Malays and Chinese. They set up wooden stakes along the shoreline that formed *kelongs* (fish farms) containing fish traps. The historical memory of the place is well-preserved in vernacular Malay, as Tanjong Pagar means 'Cape of Stakes'.

Through the passage of almost two centuries, Singapore has undergone a transformation from being a part of the Johor-Lingga Empire to a British colony, and later modern Singapore. Over this period, Tanjong Pagar has acquired a diverse sense of belonging and attachment for people of different races and religions who have lived here. The built environment thus provides distinctive identities, meanings and symbols for different localities within this area.

Mount Palmer

Sited alongside a Chinese temple is a small hill, part of a series of small coastal hill formations known as Mount Wallich and Mount Palmer that stood over 120 years ago. Travelling along Shenton Way, many are unaware that the remains of Mount Palmer are located along Palmer Road.

In the early days of the settlement of Singapore, John Palmer, a merchant from Calcutta, had purchased land in the vicinity for the construction of his house. In 1827, his house was purchased by a Parsi for use as a Parsi Club, and a section of the hill slope was used as a Parsi community burial ground.

In 1869, the colonial government constructed a military fort in this area to guard the eastern entrance to Keppel Harbour. Equipped with five 56-pound guns, Fort Palmer was to form a series of fortresses at Pasir Panjang, Pulau Blakang Mati (present-day Sentosa), Pulau Brani and Tanjong Katong for the defense of Singapore island.

Mount Wallich and a section of Mount Palmer were levelled between 1878 and 1885, and the soil used for the Telok Ayer reclamation project. Fort Palmer was subsequently demolished

between 1905 and 1915, and the soil similarly used for the second phase of the reclamation project.

Today, some of the remains of the Parsi burial ground can be seen within the secondary forest on the slope of Mount Palmer.

Fook Tet Soo Khek Temple

The Fook Tet Soo Khek Temple (*Wanghai Da Bo Gong Miao*) is Singapore's oldest Hakka temple. Constructed in 1844, this temple at Palmer Road had enjoyed what was considered excellent *feng shui*. On what was then the coastline of Tanjong Pagar, the temple had the sea fronting it while Mount Palmer backed it. Some semblance of this good *feng shui* can still be observed today with the remains of Mount Palmer at the rear and Keppel Harbour fronting the coast.

However, an earlier version of the Chinese temple built by Hakka immigrants was already sited on the shores of Tanjong Pagar when Sir Stamford Raffles founded Singapore in 1819. Hailing from the districts of Da Bu, Feng Shun, Jia Ying and Yong Ding in China, the Hakka community proceeded to renovate the temple in the succeeding years of 1844 and extended it with the addition of a

western wing in 1861 and an eastern wing (named *Tong De Gong*) in 1908.

Fook Tet Soo Khek Temple is administered jointly by the Hakka community through the Ying Fo Fui Kun (founded in 1823) and Fong Yun Thai Association (founded in 1882). Its management committee comprises members from these two Hakka clans.

Constructed in the Southern Chinese Min-nan style, this small single-storey structure comprises a main temple (*fu de ci*) and a supplementary temple (*tong de*). The main temple is dedicated to the worship of the *Tua Pek Kong* deity. Visitors would notice that both the main and supplementary temples have a rectilinear, open-to-sky courtyard. This layout is representative of the "four points of gold" (*si dian jin*) within Teochew architecture.

The roof ridge of the temple is decorated with ornaments formed by what appears to be ceramic chips pasted on clay sculptures using the *jian nian* technique of the Teochews. However, if one observes carefully, the ornaments are not made from ceramic chips. Rather, for reasons lost to history, cockle shells were pasted on the clay sculptures. This bears testament to the creativity of the builders, and makes it the only temple in Singapore to use cockle shells as part of its building material!

Keramat Habib Noh

Many have passed by this Islamic structure at Palmer Road for years without being aware of its origins and significance. Located next to the 1903-built Masjid Haji Mohammed Salleh, the Keramat Habib Noh is one of the better-known *keramats* (mausoleum of an Islamic holy man) in Singapore. This is the grave of Habib Noh bin Mohammad al-Habshi—Muslim Saint of Singapore.

Of Yemeni descent, Habib Noh settled in Singapore in 1819 having travelled from Kedah and Penang. He was said to be a descendant of the Prophet Muhammad, and was a very kind and charitable person who had an impact on many people in West, South and Southeast Asia. Indian and Arabic travellers would seek his blessings and prayers before embarking on a long journey.

The holy man passed away at the age of 78 in July 1866 at the home of Temenggong Abu Bakar in Telok Blangah. Legend has it that following his funeral ceremony, his casket could not be moved for burial until a member of the public recalled Habib Noh's wish to be buried near Mount Palmer. The *keramat* was built by Syed Mohamed bin Ahmad Alsagoff in 1890 as Habib Noh's final resting place. Pilgrims seeking intercession from Habib Noh still climb up the 49 steps to visit the *keramat*.

Keramat
Habib Noh
37 Palmer Road
(S)079424

SINGAPORE GENERAL HOSPITAL

Within the sprawling grounds of the Singapore General Hospital (SGH) are three structures significant to the medical history and heritage of Singapore in the 20th century. The Tan Teck Guan Building and College of Medicine Building represents the centre of medical education in Singapore and Malaysia for over six decades, while the Bowyer Block represents the history of medical services in Singapore.

Tan Teck Guan Building

At the turn of the 20th century, medical education was still not available in British Singapore and Malaya. In September 1904, the Straits Settlements Government accepted the petition of Tan Jiak Kim for the establishment of a medical school. Tan contributed $12,000 towards the $87,077.08 in funds raised by the Straits Chinese British Association for the school. The Straits and Federated Malay States Medical School was thus founded on 3 July 1905. It was housed in a building that previously functioned as a female lunatic asylum.

Tan Teck Guan Building
16A College Road
(S)169855

It was not until 1911 that the medical school had a brand new building. The Tan Teck Guan Building was donated by Malacca rubber tycoon Tan Chay Yan in memory of his late father Tan Teck Guan. This modest two-storey building features a Georgian and Neo-Classical façade. An ornate archway, supported by Doric Columns, embellishes the main entrance. Two historical stone plaques on the side pillars of the Tan Teck Guan Building commemorate the early work of Tan Jiak Kim and the Straits Chinese British Association in raising funds for the founding of the medical school in 1904.

The medical school's name was changed to King Edward VII Medical School in 1913 (upon receiving a $120,000 donation from the King Edward VII Memorial Fund), and subsequently amended to King Edward VII College of Medicine in 1921.

College of Medicine Building

Following approval for the construction of a new medical college building by the government, its foundation stone was laid on 6 September 1923, and the new building was officially opened on 15 February 1926 by Governor Sir Laurence Nunns Guillemard. Designed by Major P.H. Keys, the building's façade resembles a Classical Greek building. It features a colonnade of 12 Doric columns and 11 large sculptured timber doors behind it. The bas reliefs on the left and right of the colonnades allude to the allegory of healing. Prominently perched above the central doorway is a large sculptured Roman eagle encircled by a wreath. These sculptures are the work of renowned Italian sculptor Cavalieri Rudolfo Nolli.

The College of Medicine Building and Tan Teck Guan Building served as the primary tertiary institution of medical education for Singapore until 1982. Over five decades, the medical school was known as University of Malaya Medical Faculty, University of Singapore Medical Faculty and the National University of Singapore Medical Faculty. In May 1982, the medical faculty vacated the premises after moving to Kent Ridge.

Both buildings were identified for retention and restoration to prepare them for new uses. As part of the restoration of the College of Medicine Building, it was decided that a grant staircase would be added to the building. The staircase was featured in the original building plan for the College, but it was not built. The coffered ceiling of the auditorium was restored.

The Tan Teck Guan Building was restored and strengthened with the use of steel structures to replace the timber roof and second-storey timber floor. The timber window frames were replaced with identical ones. Similarly, the roof tiles were replaced with identical ones ordered from France. The original internal granite staircase and balustrades were retained, together with the brass plaque commemorating Tan Chay Yen's donation in 1911.

The College of Medicine Building and Tan Teck Guan Building were gazetted as National Monuments of Singapore on 2 December 2002. They are now occupied by the Ministry of Health, Academy of Medicine and College of Family Physicians.

Bowyer Block

The Bowyer Block Clock Tower is home to the SGH Museum. Officially opened by President S.R. Nathan on 20 May 2005, the museum's exhibits spread over two floors, displaying artefacts and medical equipment from the yesteryears, a full-sized animatronic figure of the late Professor E.S. Monteiro and milestones of the hospital's history.

Bowyer Block is also the last physical reminder of the three hospital blocks (then known as the Upper, Middle and Lower Blocks) of the 1926 SGH. It housed both first- and second-class male wards, as well as the first-class female ward. Following World War II, the hospital renamed the three wards Bowyer, Stanley and Norris, in memory of three doctors who had perished in the war. (Bowyer Block was named after chief medical officer Dr John Herbert Bowyer, who died in the aftermath of the Double Tenth incident in Singapore.)

In 1953, a new wing was added to the Bowyer Block in the form of a children's block. It was named Mistri Wing, in remembrance of its benefactor Mr Navroji Mistri who donated $1 million for its construction. The old Mistri Wing is now the Singapore Heart Centre.

Construction of the present SGH began in phases starting in 1975. To make way for the new structures, parts of the Bowyer Block were demolished. The retained sections of old Bowyer Block comprise the porch, a corridor leading to the old Mistri Wing and six wards. The SGH Museum occupies part of the porch and spine of the old Bowyer Block, while the old wards are occupied by the Medical Social Services Department, Quality Management Department, Infection Control Unit, staff clinic, staff recreation rooms and gym, medical records room and store rooms.

THIS STONE WAS LAID BY
MR. H. R. MISTRI
ON BEHALF OF HIS BROTHER, THE LATE
MR. NAVROJI RUSTOMJI MISTRI
WHO SO GENEROUSLY DONATED THIS WING
2ND MARCH 1954

PUBLIC WORKS DEPARTMENT
SINGAPORE

Bowyer Block
11 Third Hospital
Avenue (S)168751

ST JAMES POWER STATION

As you approach the bridge that leads to the island of Sentosa, you will not help but notice the presence of a three-storey brick industrial building at the shores of Telok Blangah. This building symbolises the introduction of electricity to the Telok Blangah district and the harbour docks workshops in the 20th century. It also offers an excellent example of industrial architecture in Singapore.

St James Power Station was constructed in 1927. As Singapore's first coal-fired power plant that produced electricity, it was in service for 54 years until its closure in 1981. The building underwent successful restoration and conversion for adaptive re-use in 2005 at a cost of $43 million. This two-year restoration work was guided by the Preservation of Monuments Board.

The restored building opened its doors in late 2006, and is today Singapore's largest one-stop nightlife destination with some nine bars and clubs.

St James Power Station
3 Sentosa Gateway
S(098544)

TIONG BAHRU SIT FLATS

A few years ago, the Singapore Heritage Society had proposed that Tiong Bahru's pre-war flats and shophouses within the housing estate be nominated for listing as a UNESCO World Heritage Site. While many Singaporeans did not understand the significance of this call, the Urban Redevelopment Authority acted to gazette these flats as conservation buildings.

In the 1930s, many people were still living in houses and neighbourhoods that lacked proper sanitation, electricity, street lighting and proper urban planning, but these were available in the Tiong Bahru estate. Constructed by the Singapore Improvement Trust (SIT) between 1936 and 1954 (with a lapse during the Japanese Occupation), Singapore's first experimental public housing project witnessed an Art Deco building style being employed.

Reflecting English building principles and densities that were adapted to equatorial Singapore, the SIT housing estate reflected wide spaces and symmetrical designs. Similar to the New Town found in post-war Britain, the SIT concept placed an emphasis on creating small neighbourhoods that gave individual homes maximum privacy. The flats were constructed with modern building materials such as reinforced concrete, which allowed economies of scale to be enjoyed in mass production.

These walk-up apartment buildings of three to five storeys exhibit a Streamline Moderne style (a late variant of Art Deco), and have clean architectural façades that feature rounded balconies, thin horizontal slabs and ventilation holes. Constructed on a plan that provided for open, spacious communal areas, these flats have five-foot walkways that turn into corridors, enabling accessibility to each apartment unit. Within each apartment, the layout possesses commonality as the service space (kitchen and toilet) is placed at the rear. The architectural planning also catered for a courtyard acting as an air and light well, a back lane and a spiral staircase. The common courtyard further promoted security, as residents had open views and practiced public surveillance.

Within the first 15 years of the SIT's existence, some 2,000 housing units were completed. However, under the management of the Singapore Municipality, the SIT was plagued with inadequate funding and support, and hence its accomplishments were hampered.

There were concerns with the aesthetics and design of such housing, which was not in sync with the pressing housing needs of the urban population. The SIT was subsequently replaced by a new housing authority in independent Singapore that placed greater priority on producing a mass quantity of public housing, albeit at expense of quality, in the early years of nation building.

Yet these Tiong Bahru SIT flats have displayed resilience and relevance up to the 21st century. Besides being much sought-after property in present-day Singapore, these flats have also displayed their versatility in being adapted for private and gated living.

EAST

ABDUL GAFFOOR MOSQUE

Hidden within the side road of Dunlop Street in the Little India Conservation Area is the Abdul Gaffoor Mosque, an Islamic mosque that is one of the hidden gems of this district.

First founded in 1881 by Shaik Abdul Gaffoor (who was then a chief clerk in a law firm), the mosque was established to meet the religious needs of the South Indian immigrant community that first settled in this area. This present mosque was constructed in 1907 on the site of an older mosque dating from 1846.

The current mosque began with the founding of the Dunlop Street Mosque Endowment and the acquisition of land at Dunlop Street for the building of the mosque. Shaik Abdul Gaffoor, who was one of the trustees of the Mosque Endowment, obtained permission for the construction of shophouses (which were completed in 1903) on the property. The income earned from the rental of shophouses and other structures on the site were then used to finance the construction of the mosque. In 1927, the ownership of the mosque was undertaken by the Mohammedan Advisory Board. It is currently under the management of the Majlis Ugama Islam Singapura (MUIS).

Abdul Gaffoor Mosque was gazetted as a National Monument of Singapore in 2004. In recent years, it underwent a successful restoration. The restored religious National Monument was short-listed by UNESCO for consideration of the Asia Pacific Heritage Conservation award in 2006 and 2007.

Architectural Features

The orientation of the four-cornered Islamic mosque is built to face Mecca and the building does not follow the lot lines or face Dunlop Street directly. Its prayer hall is constructed above the ground with verandahs on three sides.

The elaborate pediment located above the main entrance to the mosque is one of the unique characteristics of this building. The pediment has a sundial within it that features the 25 rays of the sunburst, illustrated with calligraphy. Flanked on both sides of the sundial are a series of pilasters and miniature columns. Each pediment is characterised by a minaret topped with an onion-shaped dome, and surmounted with a crescent moon and star.

Above the centre of the prayer hall is a hexagonal dome that is the focal point of the religious building. From its interior, the cupola is adorned with eight cinquefoil stained glass windows that allow sunlight to filter into the hall. It is also decorated with square and round calligraphic inscriptions.

Viewed from the exterior, the cupola emerges as a hexagonal dome that comprises three levels marked by Doric pilasters. The colourful stained glass windows form the first level of the dome. The second level features pilasters and capitals topped by bottleneck balusters, while at the third level are minarets (each capped with a onion-shaped dome and topped by a crescent moon and star) at the corners of the hexagonal structure.

The roof of the mosque has a parapet wall with bottle-shaped balusters. The wall is lined with a series of 22 small six-level minarets, also crowned in the template of onion-shaped dome with a crescent moon and star.

Abdul Gaffoor
Mosque

41 Dunlop Street
S(209369)

ALSAGOFF ARAB SCHOOL

Alsagoff Arab School is the oldest of six full-time Islamic schools in Singapore. Students attend classes in Islamic studies and Arabic, in addition to the standard curriculum of English, Mathematics and the Malay language.

Constructed in 1912 near to the Hajjah Fatimah Mosque, Alsagoff Arab School was the first *madrasah* (Islamic religious school) to be built in Singapore. This girls' school was founded and endowed by Syed Mohammed bin Ahmed Alsagoff, grandson of Hajjah Fatimah.

It is housed in a simple building, which has a plain two-storey design using semicircular arches, square unformed columns, an odd-shaped pediment over the portico and cast iron balustrades. The school building also features wide verandahs.

Alsagoff
Arab School

111 Jalan Sultan
S(199006)

FAMOUS ALSAGOFFS

Syed Mohammed was a successful businessman and entrepreneur. Besides trading in sago, coffee, cocoa, rubber, timber and other products with Europe and the Middle East, his business also extended into real estate, and he owned a lot of land in Singapore and southern Johor. In 1878, the Sultan of Johor granted him an agricultural concession and awarded him the right to issue his own private currency.

Syed Mohammed was a generous and charitable man who shared his immense wealth with the community. Other endowments he founded to help the community include the Syed Mohammed bin Ahmed Alsagoff (SMA) Wakaff Fund, the Muslimin Trust Fund Association of Singapore and the Muslim Boys Orphanage at Mattar Road. He had also set up a free dispensary known as the Alsagoff Dispensary.

Syed Mohammed had two roads named after him. The first, which no longer exists today, was Jalan Alsagoff, which used to stretch from Geylang Serai to Lorong Tai Seng. The second is also named Jalan Alsagoff, and is located in the town of Pontian in southern Johor.

Syed Mohammed's youngest son, Dato Syed Ahmad Alsagoff (1896–1965), also contributed much to community service. He was one of the pioneer scoutmasters of the Singapore Boy Scout Movement, and as Assistant Commissioner of the St John's Ambulance Brigade. In recognition of his community service, Queen Elizabeth II honoured him with the Member of British Empire decoration in 1953.

BIDADARI MEMORIAL GARDEN

Bidadari Cemetery was one of the oldest Singapore cemeteries, and a well-known local landmark. In use between 1907 and 1972, the cemetery had some 147,000 graves within its Muslim, Christian and Hindu burial grounds. Resting here were some of Singapore's most prominent citizens, personalities and leaders of the 20th century.

The cemetery grounds were closed for burial in 1972, and the government subsequently announced in 1996 that the site was slated for redevelopment. This sparked public concern over the loss of Bidadari's rich history, and calls were made for the retention of its memory. Bidadari Memorial Garden was hence set up at Mount Vernon Road (next to the Gurkha Police Contingent camp) by the National Heritage Board to remind present and future generations of Singapore's history and the contributions of its forefathers. While all the graves were exhumed, the memorial had a non-religious common space consisting only of the erection of some 20 selected headstones. No remains from exhumed graves were re-interned here.

Memories of the cemetery are preserved, with significant objects and structures being moved to the new site. The Bidadari Memorial Garden can be identified by the original Bidadari Cemetery gate bearing the lion emblem of the former Singapore Municipal Council.

The selected gravestones bear names of personalities such as Ahmad Ibrahim (former Minister for Health), Sir Song Ong Siang (lawyer and church leader who wrote *One Hundred Years' History of the Chinese in Singapore*), Dr Lim Boon Keng (doctor and social reformer), R.A.J. Bidwell (architect), Dato Dr Charles Joseph Pemberton Paglar (doctor, Eurasian community leader and politician), Captain Noor Mohamed Hashim bin Mohamed Dali (Singapore's first Malay/Muslim commissioned military officer and unofficial Malay member of Straits Settlements Legislative Council), Che Zahara Noor Mohamed (founder of the Malay Women's Welfare Association) and Haji Abdul Rahim Kajai (father of Malay Journalism).

Victims of the 1915 Sepoy Mutiny and the 1954 plane crash at Kallang Airport have also been commemorated in signboards placed on site, along with a memorial to British seamen. The latter addition was due to the efforts of retired merchant seamen Fred Waddington and John Bax, who had campaigned for a memorial for these seamen, and others who died during World War II and were buried at Bidadari. Amongst those were merchant seamen of old shipping companies such as Blue Funnel, Glen Lines, Straits Steamship, Royal Dutch Interocean, CP Ships and British India. Ex-servicemen, personnel of the Federation of Malaya Police who were killed during service, and others who perished in Changi's internment camp were also buried in Bidadari. The memorial plaque, cast in Australia, is donated by the Merchant Seamen Association, and placed on one of the pillars of the former Bidadari Cemetery gates.

Bidadari Memorial Garden

Mount Vernon Road

CHURCH OF THE NATIVITY OF THE BLESSED VIRGIN MARY

Constructed in 1901, this century-old religious building is the first Teochew Catholic church in Singapore. Prior to its construction, Teochew Catholics residing at Serangoon and Punggol worshipped at a brick chapel known as St Mary's Church.

The building of the Church of the Nativity of the Blessed Virgin Mary can be attributed to the efforts of Father Jean Casimir Saleilles, a Catholic parish priest serving in this district between 1881 and 1911. Father Charles Benedict Nain was the architect responsible for its Gothic design.

Father Saleilles was active in evangelising the Catholic faith in Johor. He was the founder of the Church of Our Lady of Lourdes (Johor), which is now known as the Church of the Immaculate Conception. It carries an architectural style similar to the Church of Nativity of the Blessed Virgin Mary.

At the front of the church building is a statue of the Blessed Virgin Mary. This is a gift presented by Sultan Ibrahim of Johor to the church, on account of his excellent relationship with Father Saleilles.

In January 2005, the Preservation of Monuments Board gazetted this church as a National Monument of Singapore. Religious services in the Teochew dialect continue to be conducted here.

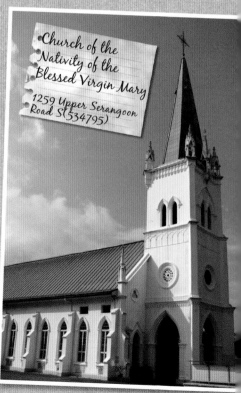

Church of the Nativity of the Blessed Virgin Mary
1259 Upper Serangoon Road S(534795)

HAJJAH FATIMAH MOSQUE

Do you know there are two National Monuments situated at opposite ends of Beach Road? At the junction of Beach Road and Bras Basah Road is the world-famous Raffles Hotel, while further down the road stands the Hajjah Fatimah Mosque, located across the St John's Ambulance Headquarters building.

The Hajjah Fatimah Mosque is the first Singapore mosque to be named after a Muslim lady—Hajjah Fatimah. Built in 1845, it was once known as the Java Road Mosque, after the street sited next to it.

According to Charles Burton Buckley in *An Anecdotal History of Old Times in Singapore 1819–1867*, Hajjah Fatimah's house at Beach Road had been attacked twice and set on fire by robbers. Hajjah Fatimah decided to construct a mosque on the site, along with several homes for the poor on the adjoining land after the second fire incident. While the mosque remains to this day, the houses for the poor have since been demolished and on this site now stands a park and the Kampong Glam Community Club.

Architectural Features

Hajjah Fatimah Mosque was designed by an English architect and the construction was executed by French contractors using Malay labour. The mosque has a single prominent minaret shaped like the tower and spire of a church. Amidst much speculation, the steeple-like minaret and the earliest parts of the mosque are believed to have been built by John Turnbull Thomson, a government surveyor.

The minaret has four levels, each decreasing in size. The first level is square-shaped, with each side having a recessed arch framed by twin pilasters with Doric capitals. There is a sacred heart motif beneath the arch and a circular opening surrounded by heavy moulding in the centre. The second level is octagonal, and each corner is ornamented with a round pilaster flanked by two flat pilasters with Doric capitals as well. The third level echoes the design of the second, but on a smaller scale; and the fourth level is an elongated pyramid with an octagonal base. The pyramid is capped with three spheres of decreasing size ending in an arrow.

Hajjah Fatimah
Mosque

4001 Beach Road
S(199584)

The mosque's "tower and spire" also tilts at an angle of about six degrees, making it Singapore's very own "leaning tower". Though corrective works were implemented in 1970s to correct this, it appears that the tower has continued to tilt.

The imam's residence in the premises was formerly the residence of Hajjah Fatimah. It is a two-storey building characterised by roof eaves edged with open timber fretwork, and timber-louvered casement windows. The corners and bays of the house are marked out by moulded pilasters. They have Doric capitals and mouldings in mid-shaft.

Located within the mosque's grounds are also the tombs of Hajjah Fatimah, her daughter Raja Siti and son-in-law Syed Ahmed Alsagoff. The mausoleum carries a traditional Islamic design, and its roof parapet features merlon cresting. The casement windows have lancet-shaped arches with coloured glass, and are of the same design as the windows on the onion-shaped dome. Outside the mausoleum is a small cemetery where Hajjah Fatimah's family members are buried.

JAPANESE CEMETERY

Nestled along Chuan Hoe Avenue off Yio Chu Kang Road is a 130-year-old Japanese cemetery. The 910 tombstones and markers in this small cemetery represent the community experience of the Japanese in Singapore dating from the late-19th century to present times. There are a few phases in this historical development.

The Karayuki-San (1870–1920)

The earliest Japanese tombstones in this cemetery are those of young Japanese women from poor families who were prostitutes in the port of Singapore. Known as *karayuki-san*, these teenage women worked in Japanese-run brothels, which then dominated the sex industry in the booming ports around the Asia-Pacific region. They remitted their earnings back to their families in Japan, indirectly helping their country's economic development with their foreign currency remittances. In 1887, there were more than 100 Japanese prostitutes working in a handful of brothels. By 1905, Singapore had 109 brothels with over 630 Japanese prostitutes.

The Japanese Cemetery was founded in 1891 by a Japanese brothel owner, Tagajiro Futaki, as a burial ground for the young women who died without family or kin in Singapore. This early *karayuki* cemetery was characterised by wooden grave markers. With the passage of time, these wooden markers were replaced with tombstones erected by the Kyosaikai (Mutual Self Help Society). These tombstones can still be seen in the cemetery.

The graves of the *karayuki-san* are placed at the eastern corner of the cemetery, opposite a Buddhist temple (Saiyuji) located right at the other extreme end. Such an arrangement starkly reflects the low social position of the *karayuki-san*, that even in death, they are deemed to be an ethnic shame, far removed from Buddhist religious norms and beliefs.

The Japanese Middle Class (1920–1941)

In the first decades of the 20th century, Singapore witnessed the emergence of a Japanese middle class that altered the demographic

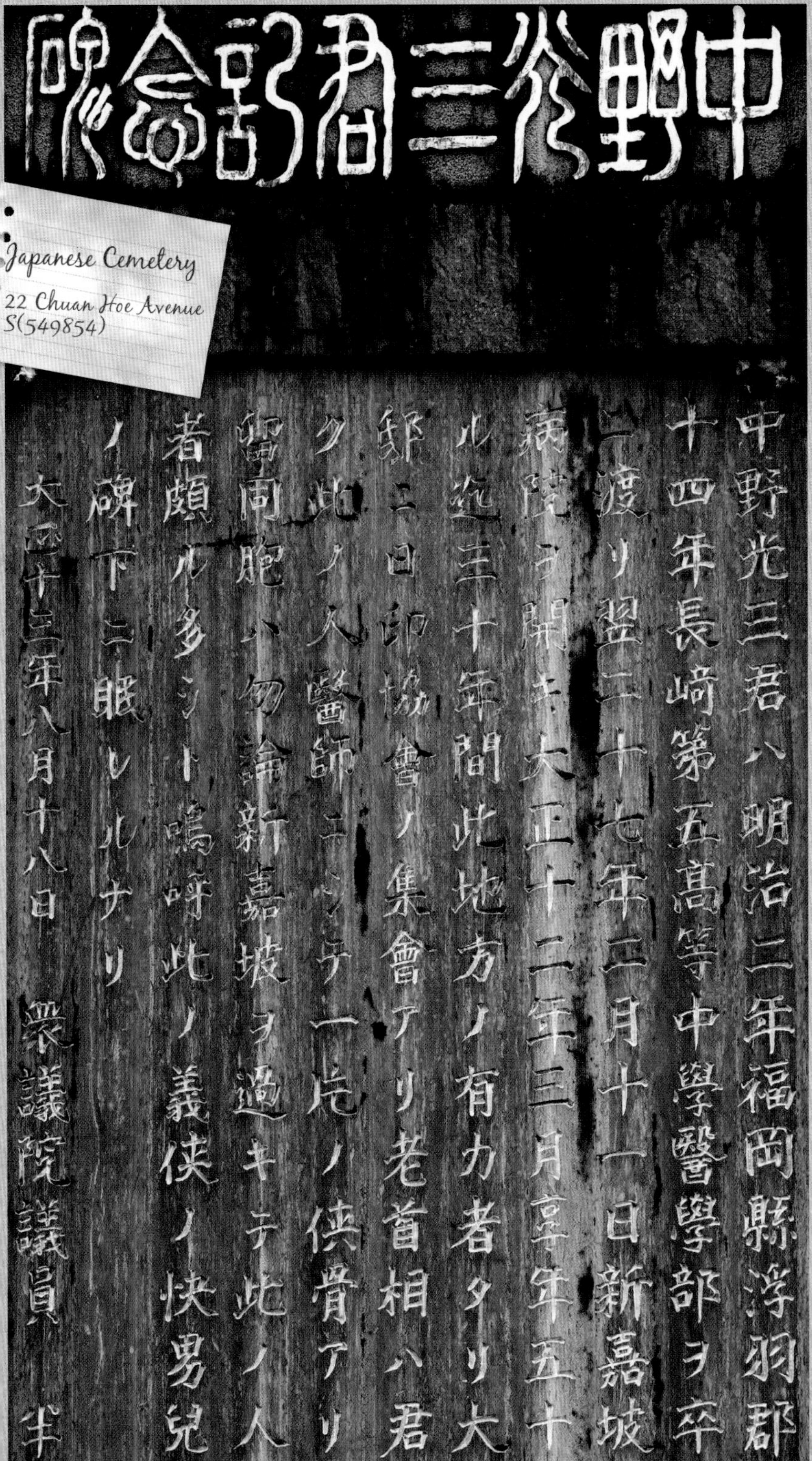
中野光三君記念碑
中野光三君ハ明治二年福岡縣浮羽郡
十四年長崎第五高等中學醫學部ヲ卒
ニ渡リ翌二十七年二月十一日新嘉坡
病院ヲ開キ大正十二年三月享年五十
ル迄三十年間此地方ノ有力者タリ大
邦ニ日印協會ノ集會アリ老首相ハ君
ク此ノ人醫師ニシテ一片ノ侠骨アリ
當同胞ハ勿論新嘉坡ヲ過キテ此ノ人
者頗ル多シト嗚呼此ノ義侠ノ快男兒
ノ碑下ニ眠レルナリ
大正十二年八月十八日 衆議院議員 半
Japanese Cemetery
22 Chuan Hoe Avenue
S(549854)

profile of the Singapore Japanese community. Japan had sought to repatriate the *karayuki-san* back to their homeland, and in their place, a new Japanese community sought to increase Japanese economic activities here. These included the opening of Japanese banks and Japanese-owned godowns in the port. As such, this new class of Japanese migrants was known as the *gudan-zoku* (godown people).

Japanese schools were also set up for their children. Furthermore, the Japanese Association, founded in 1915, quickly became the de facto Japanese community association in Singapore. It assumed management of the Japanese Cemetery, where the *karayuki* heritage of yesteryear was replaced by the middle class that had established their dominance with the placement of their burial spots. This marked the shift of the cemetery towards a middle-class appearance, characterised by larger and more sophisticated tombstones.

The Japanese Invasion and Occupation of Singapore (1942–1945)

The Japanese perception of World War II is represented in the Japanese Cemetery, which was expanded to become an informal military cemetery after the war.

During the Japanese Occupation, the Japanese military administration had sought to honour their soldiers who lost their lives in the Malayan campaign by setting up a 12-metre tall pillar as a war monument (Syonan Chureito at Bukit Batok) and a Shinto war shrine (Syonan Jinja at MacRitchie Reservoir). Following the unconditional Japanese surrender in 1945, these structures were destroyed by the Japanese military.

During the post-war years, however, commemoration of the Japanese war dead was carried out by Japanese servicemen in the Japanese Cemetery. The cremated remains of army and naval personnel were relocated from the Syonan Chureito and elsewhere to a memorial set up in the cemetery. Other memorials on the grounds include the memorial for martyrdom of patriots (Junna Resshi No Hi), which remembers Japanese servicemen who had committed suicide after the surrender and servicemen executed as war criminals, and a memorial to Field Marshall Count Terauchi, supreme commander of the Japanese army in Southeast Asia. Located near to the Junna Resshi No Hi are monuments commemorating Japanese war criminals hanged at Changi and in Malaya. These structures were erected between 1946 and 1947.

KAMPONG KAPOR METHODIST CHURCH

Beginning as a prayer group started by the missionary Miss Sophia Blackmore in 1890, the church became known as the Malay Church when it moved to the Christian Institute at Middle Road in 1894. Under the leadership of Reverend William Shellabear, this Malay language vernacular church reached out and evangelised to the Straits Chinese community. Over time, the church congregation reflected a Straits Chinese membership.

In 1930, the expanded church moved to a new building at Kampong Kapor Road. It became known as the Straits Chinese Methodist Church (Bickley Memorial), in recognition of monetary donations and contributions by the family and friends of Bishop Bickley.

The church was renamed Kampong Kapor Methodist Church in 1957 and celebrated its centenary in 1994. Today, the building has been conserved.

Kampong Kapor
Methodist Church

1 Kampong Kapor Road
S(208673)

MALABAR MOSQUE

The Malabar Mosque was built as a place of religious worship by Malabar Muslim immigrants (from the Indian state of Kerala). The mosque was constructed by the Malabar Muslim Jamaath (founded in 1927), a social association that was active in providing for the social and religious needs of the Malabar Muslims.

The foundation stone for Singapore's first Malabar Mosque was laid on 10 April 1956, but its construction took over six years to complete as it was dependent on an ongoing fund-raising campaign to finance the building project. The mosque was officially opened by Singapore's *Yang Di-Pertuan Negara* (Head of State) Yusof Ishak on 24 January 1963.

Since then, the Malabar Mosque has been the focal point of the Malabar Muslims who pray there. It contributes to the community's identity and sense of heritage with the observation of religious and social events. At the back of the mosque is an old burial ground. Dating back to 1819, this burial space is used by the Malabar Muslims.

Malabar Mosque
471 Victoria Street
S(198370)

Architectural Features

The compound consists of the main mosque and an octagonal tower that serves as the calling tower. These structures are topped by a series of onion-shaped domes with a crescent moon and a star at the pinnacle. On the elevated first floor is the prayer hall that is surrounded with verandahs on three sides. It is oriented towards Mecca. At ground level are spaces used for the study of the *Qu'ran*, an imam's room, visitors' lounge and storage facilities. The lower and upper floors are connected by external staircases.

The mosque took on its current green-and-blue façade when it was tiled in 1995.

OLD FORT TANJONG KATONG

Situated within present-day Katong Park are the remains of Old Fort Tanjong Katong. Constructed by the Straits Settlements Government as part of coastal fortification works to defend Singapore, this 130-year-old British fort is amongst the oldest built defensive structures left from the 19th century. It was commissioned by the British War Office, and constructed at a cost of $4,200.

In 1879, the British did not recognise the Treaty of San Stefano signed by Russia and the Ottoman Empire, in which the Russians sought to expand their maritime activities by seeking unrestricted passage rights through seas. The British responded to this perceived threat by building and equipping the fort with coastal guns in this then remote and rural corner of the island to protect Singapore against perceived Russian invaders. However, the Russian military threat did not materialise. Other factors contributing to the obsolete nature of the fort include the improvement in military technology and weaponry, as well as the lack of personnel to man the fort. Furthermore, the fort's remote location created logistical problems for personnel reinforcements and military supplies. The British military planners eventually made the decision to abandon the fort in 1901 by burying it under tons of earth.

In the ensuing years, the land was used as a public recreational space, culminating in the creation of a public park in the late 1920s.

Memory of the old fort gradually faded from public consciousness over the course of the century. The sea facing Katong Park was lost after land reclamation at East Coast commenced in the 1960s, and the name of the adjacent road—Fort Road—was the only reminder that a fort was once here.

Old Fort
Tanjong Katong

Katong Park,
Fort Road

Discovery of the remains of the old fort came about from archaeo-logical research conducted on site by Professor John Miksic, Mr Lim Chen Sian and undergraduates from the Department of Southeast Asian Studies at the National University of Singapore during the academic year of 2004–2005. With the support of the Mountbatten Citizens' Consultative Committee, the archaeological project, *Raising History, Planting Roots*, revealed much of the old fort's foundation. This included a large section of the perimeter wall, two infantry bastions at the edge of the fort and the remains of a drawbridge.

Following this excavation, the exposed remains of the trenches of the old fort were backfilled with sand in order to protect them from weather elements and looters, and to keep them intact for future archaeological studies, as well as for public safety.

OLD KALLANG AIRPORT TOWER

Opened in 1937, Kallang Airport was Singapore's first civilian airport which boasted an airfield and a slipway for seaplanes. Prior to this, the Royal Air Force's (RAF) Seletar Airbase had a secondary function of serving commercial airlines that transited in Singapore en route to Australia, New Zealand, Indonesia, Middle East and Europe. However, congestion at Seletar Airbase resulted in the decision to construct a commercial airport at Kallang Basin, dedicated to servicing the booming commercial aviation industry.

Work on the new civilian airport took place between 1932 and 1937. It involved the reclamation of the Kallang Basin and building of an airport terminal and control tower, runway and a slipway for seaplanes to be served by the main airport terminal.

During World War II, the airport became a fighter airfield for the RAF. Squadrons of the RAF, Royal New Zealand Air Force and the Royal Netherlands East Indies Air Force defended Singapore from this airfield until Singapore fell to the Japanese. It was then used by the Japanese air force during the Japanese Occupation.

In post-war Singapore, Kallang Airport reverted to civilian use. Regular flights resumed between Europe, Australia, New Zealand and

Southeast Asia. Post-war technological advancements witnessed the growth in aircraft sizes and the need for more space for airplanes to land and take off, as well as to be docked. The Kallang Basin lacked the area required to support this expansion, and thus a decision was made to construct a new airport at Paya Lebar in 1951.

Kallang Airport was closed when Paya Lebar Airport became operational on 20 August 1955. The former was converted for new use as the headquarters of the People's Association (PA), and this remained so for the next five decades until the PA's move to Prince George's Avenue. The building is currently vacant.

Architectural Features

The completed Kallang Airport Terminal building was unlike any other in Singapore during the 1930s. Designed by Frank Dorrington Ward, chief architect of the Public Works Department, the two-storey building had a large open-air viewing gallery on the second storey and a circular control tower in the middle. This building is amongst the Art Deco masterpieces of the 1930s that can still be found in the country. This building's architecture sought to represent the technological advancement of aviation and to express the rapid speed in which civilisation was being transformed by planes and air travel, as seen in the bold use of clean lines and geometric forms in its design. Outstretched wings of the building and the cantilevered balconies symbolise the airplane. The use of exposed concrete, horizontal lines, transparent glazed walls and streamline curves manifest the expression of the architectural language of functionalism.

Old Kallang
Airport Tower

9 Stadium Link,
S(397750)

SRI PERUMAL TEMPLE

Dating back to the early days of Singapore when it was administered by the East Indian Company, a group of Indian community leaders pooled together their resources and purchased a two-acre plot of land for 26 rupees and 8 annas. This land, sited at present-day Serangoon Road near Race Course Road, was used to build the Narasinga Perumal Kovil temple for Vaishnavite worship in 1855. Renamed the Sri Srinivas Perumal Temple, the temple is dedicated to the worship of the Hindu deity Lord Perumal, and believers come here to seek his blessings.

A gazetted National Monument of Singapore, the temple's entrance tower (*gopuram*) was rebuilt and reinstated in the early 1960s by P. Govindasamy Pillay, a wealthy Indian businessman. Mr Pillay continued to lend his support by financing the restoration and repair costs of the temple, as well as the addition of a marriage hall in the 1970s. The temple remains well-maintained, with regular restoration work taking place during the 1980s and 1990s. The most recent restoration took place in 2005.

Visitors to the temple would be greeted by the magnificent five-tiered *gopuram* that is decorated with Hindu deities. Within the temple's compound, one can see the well laid-out sanctums exhibiting finely-sculptured embellishments. The columns in the main hall have figures of the *yaali*, an animal resembling a lion.

This temple is well-known in Singapore as the site for the start of the annual Thaipusam festival. Having undergone a preparation period of fasting and abstinence, devotees of the deity Murugan would carry *kavadis* (burdens) at this temple, and begin their journey on foot towards the direction of the Thandayuthapani Temple at Tank Road. The *kavadis* are characterised by the use of skewers that pierce a cheek, or more intricate forms utilising many skewers to pierce the bodies of the devotees. The devotees carry their *kavadis* as a test of their religious faith.

Besides Thaipusam, Sri Perumal Temple also celebrates the major Hindu festivals: Navarathiri, Vaikunda Ekathesi and Purattasi Sani.

Sri Perumal
Temple

397 Serangoon
Road S(218123)

SULTAN MOSQUE

The Sultan Mosque is the highlight of the Kampong Glam district. It is named after Sultan Hussain, Sultan of Singapore who resided in the area in 1819. The current building was constructed over a span of four years from 1924 to replace the earlier Masjid Sultan, built in 1826.

Designed by Denis Santry from the architectural firm Swan & MacLaren, Sultan Mosque was Singapore's largest mosque when it was completed in 1928, and was able to accommodate more than 4,000 worshippers during prayers.

Many have mistakenly thought the mosque's entrance to be at North Bridge Road, due to its impressive onion-shaped dome facing the road. In actual fact, this belongs to the mausoleum at the back of the mosque, which holds the burial places of Tunku Alam and Tunku Abdul Jalil (descendants of Sultan Hussain) and their wives. The main dome is located at the entrance in front of Muscat Street.

These magnificent domes are the dominant characteristic of Sultan Mosque. If you were to observe the base of the two large domes carefully, you would notice that the ornamentation band of green is made up of bottles! During the mosque's construction, many poor families living in the neighbourhood could only offer old soya sauce bottles towards the building effort, and their contributions are thus reflected in the ornamentation band.

Sultan Mosque has a special place within the Singapore Muslim community—not only is it a principal venue of worship, it is also symbolic of their unity and solidarity.

The mosque was gazetted as a Singapore National Monument on 14 March 1975.

Architectural Features

Sultan Mosque's architecture is that of the Islamic Saracenic style, which evolved from British India. This style sought to merge traditional Islamic and Indian architecture, and was popularly used in the construction of official

buildings in India. In his architectural design, Denis Santry sought to combine Indian architectural heritage with British utility and standards.

The gold-coloured dome roofs are each flanked by four Doric columns with square bases. The domes are also topped by pinnacles with crescent moons and stars and surrounded with cupolas. The roof parapet features 40 miniature minaret-like towers.

The mosque interior consists of 12 large columns within two rows. There are eight equally-spaced bays of arches that frame the inside of the prayer hall along both the northern and southern sections. Balconies are located above to provide additional prayer space.

Sultan Mosque

3 Muscat Street
S(198833)

SULTAN OF SINGAPORE PALACE
(Istana Kampong Glam)

Kampong Glam was the traditional seat of the Singapore's Malay Royalty (*Kerajaan*) prior to the arrival of the British on Singapore's shores in February 1819. Named after the Gelam tree, this district had an existing settlement pre-dating the British. Raffles' 1822 Master Plan recognised the existing settlement by zoning it for occupation by the Malays, Bugis and Arabs. It was also reserved for Sultan Hussain Shah (Sultan of Singapore) and his descendants.

The beginnings of modern Singapore were planted when Sultan Hussain signed the 6 February 1819 treaty with Sir Stamford Raffles to allow the British to set up a factory and establishment on the island. Within a few years, British dominance stripped the Sultan of all his political powers. On 2 August 1824, Sultan Hussain had no choice but to accept the proposals of Resident John Crawfurd to cede Singapore to the British. This cemented British control over Singapore.

A significant landmark associated with the royalty in Kampong Glam is the former Istana of the Sultan of Singapore. On the southeastern corner of this compound stands a two-storey house featuring a Palladian architectural style, constructed in 1840 by Sultan Hussain's son, Sultan Ali. Believed to be the work of architect G.D. Coleman, it was occupied by the Sultan's family and descendants for the next 150 years. Archaeological excavations undertaken on this site between 2000 and 2003 uncovered remains of a pre-1840 structure that Sultan Hussain might have lived in.

The decades following 1840 witnessed British efforts to terminate the Malay sultanate of Kampong Glam. Sultan Ali and his successor Tunku Abdul Jalil yielded their sovereign rights of Johor (in 1855) and Muar respectively. Henceforth, the descendants of the Singapore sultanate never exercised sovereignty over any territories. In 1897, fortunes of Sultan Hussain's descendants took a further dip when the Straits Settlements Court of Appeal ruled that the Kampong Glam land belonged to the colony of Singapore.

Descendants of Sultan Hussain moved out of Istana Kampong Glam in 1999 after reaching a settlement with the Government of Singapore, in which they would receive a total allowance of $350,000 per annum for 30 years beginning 1 March 2000.

Located at the left-hand side of the Istana's gate post is a large two-storey mansion known as the Gedong Kuning (Yellow Mansion), which was built by Tunku Mahmoud (son of Sultan Ali) as his residence. After his death, the house was sold. It later became the family home of Haji Yusoff, a belt maker and successful entrepreneur. His family lived in the house from 1912 to 1989.

Istana Kampong Glam and the Gedong Kuning have been restored. The former is now the Malay Heritage Centre under the management of the National Heritage Board, while the latter is a Malay restaurant known as Tepak Sireh Restoran. This venue is popular for cultural performances and weddings.

Sultan of
Singapore Palace

85 Sultan Gate
S(198501)

TOU MU KUNG TEMPLE

Along Upper Serangoon Road is a small Chinese Taoist temple that bears the name of Tou Mu Kung—Goddess of the North Star and Mother of the Nine Emperors. Within the Chinese Taoist order of deities, she ranks higher than the celestial emperors and is thus honoured by devotees. However, the Goddess is not the deity worshipped in this temple, but rather the Nine Emperors. Hence, this temple is also known by its other name—*Kew Ong Yah* (in Hokkien) or *Kau Wong Yeh* (in Cantonese).

Constructed in 1921, the origins of the temple can be attributed to Hokkien businessman Ong Choo Kee. While in Penang on a business trip in 1902, he made a personal pledge of devotion to the Nine Emperors should his business ventures be fruitful. Shortly after, he indeed experienced success in his business, and reciprocated by installing an amulet of the Nine Emperors at his family altar. Some years later, Ong had a dream in which an old man instructed him to build a temple to honour the Nine Emperors at Upper Serangoon Road. Ong followed the instructions and began its construction in 1919, becoming the founder of this temple.

Since its founding, the temple has served as an ancestral temple of the Ong family, where ancestral tablets are kept. A permanent *wayang* (opera) stage was further erected on the temple compound to hold Chinese theatrical performances. This structure was a landmark of the Serangoon district for seven decades until its demolition in 1998 to facilitate the expansion of Upper Serangoon Road.

The main religious event of this temple is the observation of the birthday of the Nine Emperors. Held during the first to the ninth day of the ninth lunar month, many followers from Singapore, Malaysia and Southeast Asia would converge at the temple to celebrate this event. The followers have to observe a strict vegetarian diet for the period. Public possessions of the Nine Emperors would take place beginning with receiving the arrival of the deities from the coast on the first day, and finishing with the sending-off parade of the deities at the end of the nine days. Chinese theatrical performances would also be held on the temple's grounds.

In addition to the Nine Emperors, other Taoist deities—The Empress Register of Births and Goddess Kuan Yin—are also worshipped at this temple. The Tou Mu occupies a prominent place within both Chinese Buddhism and Taoism. While Tou Mu Kung Temple is predominantly a Taoist Temple, it also features Buddhist influences, and can hence be characterised as a syncretic temple.

For eight decades, Tou Mu Kung Temple was continuously managed by the descendants of Ong Choo Kee until recent years, when management was transferred to the Singapore Taoist Federation. As a gazetted National Monument of Singapore, this is the first *Kew Ong Yah* temple to be designated as a protected building within Southeast Asia. The Singapore Taoist Federation is currently preparing for the restoration of the temple and the construction of a new *wayang* stage within the temple's grounds.

Tou Mu Kung Temple

779A Upper Serangoon Road S(534648)

BUKIT TIMAH NATURE RESERVE

The attention that Bukit Timah Nature Reserve commands is disproportionate to its modest land area of 163 hectares (1.63 sq km). Families craving a day out together, mountaineers training for Himalayan expeditions and tourists fresh from a downtown shopping spree all converge on Bukit Timah, whose stature as the highest ground in Singapore at 164 metres above sea level in no way detracts from its antidotal effects on urbanisation.

Struggling up the "mother of all slopes", one can only gasp breathlessly or be breath-taken—or both—at the cathedral of towering dipterocarps (family name of the trees which dominate Bukit Timah) whose canopy blots out the sun at more than 30 metres above the forest floor. This is the very place where, over a century before, Alfred Russel Wallace—the person who stood shoulder to shoulder with Charles Darwin—collected specimens for research on his own version of the theory of natural selection.

Privy to most scrutinising observers is a spectacular array of swimming, crawling and flying creatures sharing an intimate relationship with Bukit Timah's forest, which boasts more plant species than the entire continent of North America. However, as one *National Geographic* maxim goes, the only constant is change, and it would be for the worse unless Man reversed his trajectory on a planetary scale. In Bukit Timah Nature Reserve, the imprint of Man has been manifested in the forest's fragmentation and desiccation, and reinforced by the visibility of skyscrapers through thin foliage on the higher slopes. The endemic freshwater crab *Johora Singaporensis*, unique to this country, has been found no less susceptible to today's environmental metastasis than what the fragility of its last refuge of crystalline streams in Bukit Timah suggests.

This rainforest's kinship with the Malay Peninsula goes deeper than biodiversity. As mountain ranges rose skywards eons ago to form the spine of the peninsula, they tapered off into bumps at the southern end. One of these bumps came to be known as Bukit Timah Hill. The granite of which the hill is composed was strong and amenable to structural exploitation—tunnels dug by invading Japanese forces for ammunition storage during World War II was followed by large-scale post-war mining of granite. Ironically, the quarries that had eaten away the hillsides now add to the scenic beauty and, on one or two occasions, freshwater biodiversity of the area.

The main path to Bukit Timah Hill's summit was built in 1843, before the hill was designated as a forest reserve 40 years later. With the Nature Reserves Ordinance of 1951, Bukit Timah Nature Reserve was accorded greater protection. The National Parks Board now manages the reserve under the Parks and Trees Act 2005.

Bukit Timah
Nature Reserve
177 Hindhere Drive,
(S) 589333

CHINESE HIGH SCHOOL CLOCK TOWER

The Chinese High School clock tower is a prominent landmark in Bukit Timah. At about three storeys high, one can easily tell the time on the tower, even from a bus travelling along Bukit Timah Road. The clock tower stands in the middle of a T-shaped structure, with a wing of classrooms on its left and right sides and an assembly hall in front of it. This is the Tower Block.

As part of Chinese High School's original buildings since 1925, the clock tower has been a silent witness of the school's long history. It began when well-known Singapore-Chinese businessman and philanthropist Tan Kah Kee became President of the Singapore Hokkien Huay Kuan, and worked with the clan association members to promote modern Chinese education in Singapore. They started the Singapore Nanyang Hua Chiao Middle School on 21 March 1919 at 15 Niven Road (near Selegie Centre), with an enrolment of 78 students.

As President of the School Management Board, Tan Kah Kee was one of the early supporters who helped to raise funds to purchase the land for the new school site in May 1919 at a cost of $83,000 Straits Settlement dollars, (approximately $8.3 million in present-day value). This amount did not include construction costs.

The school relocated to its present site at Bukit Timah Road in 1925 and became known as the Chinese High School. The landmark clock tower was also constructed in the same year and designed by Frank Lundon from the firm Swan & MacLaren, which also designed the Victoria Memorial Hall and Raffles Hotel. Covering 79 acres (0.32 sq km) of land, the campus is one of the biggest secondary school compounds in Singapore.

In 1979, Chinese High School became one of the first local schools to participate in the Special Assistance Plan (SAP), whereby students undertook English and Chinese as first languages. The school became independent in 1988.

Over the past eight decades, there have been numerous improvements to the school campus. Its students now enjoy the use of facilities such as a drama centre, art centre, gymnasium, amphitheatre, swimming pool and a full-sized football field encircled by a

400-metre running track. The school continues to excel in providing good education for its students.

Generations of students have passed through the gates of Chinese High School. Its graduates, both famous and infamous, include the late Ong Teng Cheong (who was Deputy Prime Minister and President of Singapore), Lim Chin Siong (founder-member of the People's Action Party), Malayan Communist Party leader Fang Chuang Pi (better known as "The Plen") and opposition politician Tan Liang Hong.

Without the efforts of pioneers such as Tan Kah Kee whose philanthropy made the school a reality, many would have been denied access to education. In commemoration of his contribution, a multi-purpose hall on the school campus was named the Kah Kee Hall in his honour. President Ong Teng Cheong officiated at its official opening as part of the school's 75th anniversary celebration in 1994.

The clock tower was officially gazetted as a National Monument on 19 March 1999.

Chinese High School Clock Tower

673 Bukit Timah Road S(269735)

TAN KAH KEE (1874–1961)

Born in Jimei, Fujian Province, China, Tan Kah Kee left his hometown in search of a better life in Singapore when he was only 16 years old. His father had taught him commerce and the trading of rice. After a few years, Tan set up his own business and ventured into the pineapple-canning business. He successfully set up a canning plant in 1910, as well as his own pineapple plantations. Following this early success, he diversified into the rubber industry. His rubber business thrived, and he became known as the "Rubber King" of Southeast Asia in 1925.

Tan is remembered for his lifelong effort in promoting Chinese education in Singapore and China. His work as President of the Hokkien Huay Kuan witnessed the founding of three primary schools and two high schools in Singapore, including the Chinese High School. Furthermore, Tan promoted English education and donated funds to the Anglo-Chinese School and Raffles College (the predecessor of the National University of Singapore).

His greatest contribution to education though was the founding of Amoy University at Xiamen, Fujian Province, in 1921. This was the first private Chinese university to be founded by an overseas Chinese, and is now a prestigious national university in China.

In 1950, Tan returned to China for his retirement. When he passed away in Beijing in 1961 at 87 years old, the Chinese Government accorded him a state funeral.

COMMAND HOUSE

Just off Bukit Timah Road, opposite the NUS Bukit Timah campus, is the Command House sited on a 4.7-hectare (47,000 sqm) site. First known as Flagstaff House when it was completed in 1939, the two-storey house was the official residence of the General Officer of Commanding Local Forces in the British colonial era. The first two British generals to reside here were Major-General W.G.S. Dobbie and Lieutenant-General A.E. Percival. After the war, the British Military Administration took possession of the house. During this period, it served as the residence of Admiral Lord Louis Mountbatten, Supreme Allied Commander, Southeast Asia Command.

From 1947 to 1971, 13 succeeding military commanders comprising Generals, Admirals and Air Chief Marshals continued to reside at the house—renamed the Command House—until the British military's withdrawal from Singapore in 1971. The building was handed over to the Singapore government that year, whence it became the official residence of the Speaker of Parliament, Dr Yeoh Ghim Seng. Dr Yeoh occupied the house until January 1989. The succeeding Speaker of Parliament, Mr Tan Soo Khoon, however, did not continue with the tradition of staying in the Command House.

The house was then used by President Ong Teng Cheong for state functions during his term as the fifth President of the Republic of Singapore. Activities that took place here during this period included presenting appointment instruments to Nominated MPs, administering the oath of office to new Ministers, acceptance of credentials of new ambassadors and high commissioners to Singapore, and hosting of dinners and luncheons.

Command House has now been restored and converted for its new use as the UBS Asia-Pacific Wealth Management campus. UBS AG conducts specialised training for its staff from the Asia-Pacific region in this building.

The house was shortlisted by UNESCO as a Singapore finalist for the 2008 UNESCO Asia-Pacific Heritage Building Conservation award.

Architectural Features

Located in a large garden setting atop a small hill with generous lawns and surrounding greenery, Command House's Arts and Crafts architectural style has features that include: a long symmetrical double-storey layout with protruding carriage porch; homely appearance; double suntrap plan; pitched tiled roof; and frank expression of materials. The house was built at the height of Frank Brewer's (1886–1971) architectural influence in the 1930s. Its exposed brick arches, roughcast plaster rendering of the upper storey and slight roof upturn at the eaves constitute a gentler reading of the Arts and Crafts tradition as compared to the more boisterous flourishes seen in another Brewer-designed house at nearby 1 Dalvey Estate.

Command House
17 Kheam Hock Road
S(298791)

KRANJI WAR CEMETERY

Built in a former war zone by the Imperial War Graves Commission, the Kranji War Cemetery is Singapore's largest military commemorative structure. During the early days of the Japanese invasion of Singapore, many Allied soldiers and Singapore combatants of the Dalforce unit fought hand-to-hand against the Japanese at Woodlands, Kranji and Bukit Timah. This Kranji site served as a temporary cemetery, but grew during the Occupation when a prisoner-of-war (POW) camp and hospital were established here, and eventually became the final resting place of the Allied troops killed in fighting.

Designed by British architect Colin St Clair Oakes, the cemetery comprises several components. The Chinese Memorial is a collective grave for 69 servicemen who were killed by the Japanese in February 1942. The Singapore Memorial commemorates 24,000 military casualties with no known graves, and contains the most names amongst all Commonwealth commemorative structures in the Far East. The Singapore Cremation Memorial honours approximately 789 casualties (mostly Indian soldiers) whose remains were cremated according to their religious beliefs, and their names are recorded on the memorial beneath this inscription: "In honour of these officers and men who died in battle and whose mortal remains were committed to fire". The Singapore Civil Hospital Grave Memorial commemorates more than 400 civilians and military casualties killed by Japanese soldiers at the Singapore General Hospital during the Japanese invasion, while the Singapore (Unmaintainable Graves) Memorial remembers more than 250 casualties who died in campaigns in Singapore and Malaya, but whose known graves in civil cemeteries could not be assured maintenance, or could not be moved to Kranji on religious grounds.

The Cross of Sacrifice is the central focus of the cemetery, and reflects Britain's Anglican and Methodist background. (The Cross, which is also found at all Commonwealth cemeteries, is intended to symbolise Christian soldiers 'crucified on the battlefield'.) This Cross is based on Sir Reginald Blomfield's design and is set on an octagonal base bearing a bronze sword upon the shaft. The cemetery also features the Lutyens' Stone of Remembrance and a monument to the missing.

Remains of 4,458 military servicemen and women from Britain, Australia, Canada, Sri Lanka, India, Malaya, Singapore, the Netherlands and New Zealand are buried in this cemetery constructed in the form of a typical British war cemetery in an English country landscape. Its layout adheres faithfully to the rules of the Imperial War Graves Commission, which stipulates that each of the dead should be commemorated individually by name on headstone or memorial; that the headstones and memorials should be permanent; that the headstones should be uniform; and that there should be no distinction made on account of military or civil rank, race or creed. English is the dominant language used on the headstones, indirectly indicating the soldiers' commitment and allegiance to England.

These tombstones are set in perfectly straight rows, and carry identical dimensions. Each headstone has a slight curve at the crown, and the top is engraved with the national emblem or service or regimental badge of the deceased. This is followed by the deceased's rank, name, unit, date of death, age and appropriate religious emblem. The uniform white headstone conveys the message of the indomitable male military spirit and discipline that epitomises the British Lion. Organised in a square formation of 100 headstones (five rows of 20 headstones each), it forms a battalion when the 36 formations are seen in their entirety. The use of the garden template for the cemetery also made it necessary for non-English soldiers to be buried in this English manner. It negates the divergent identities of Commonwealth soldiers and the involvement of their countries.

Since the official unveiling of Kranji War Cemetery by Governor Sir Robert Black on 2 March 1957, the Commonwealth War Graves Commission (which changed its name in 1960 to reflect changing times) has been steadfast in not repatriating the World War II remains of Commonwealth soldiers.

Any new discoveries are buried in Kranji. As a rule, only British and Commonwealth personnel who died in the war are eligible for burial here. However, exceptions have been made. In 1975, the Kranji Military Cemetery was created on the western slope by the Commission to allow the relocation of non-World War I and II graves. This was prompted by the closure of the British military cemeteries at Pasir Panjang and Ulu Pandan in 1971 due to the Singapore Government's redevelopment plans of the rural districts. Within this section of Kranji are two small Gardens of Remembrance to commemorate the British and Gurkha servicemen, as well as their families. The gravestones are in an array of designs that reflect the military, the civilian, multi-faith and multi-ethnic character of the Ulu Pandan and Pasir Panjang cemeteries.

Military re-burials from World War I can also be found at Kranji. These are remains of soldiers killed in the 1915 Sepoy Mutiny. These gravestones are those of the Commission's 'common issue' and the remains were relocated from Bidadari Christian Cemetery in 1957. In 2001, the Office of Australian War Graves identified three graves from Bidadari Cemetery to be re-buried at Kranji.

Kranji War Cemetery

9 Woodlands Road S(738656)

OLD ADMIRALTY HOUSE

Beginning in the 1920s when the Royal Navy first started surveying work for the British naval base within the district of Sembawang in northern Singapore, planning was made for the construction of residences in this area. This included providing a house designated as an official residence for the Commodore Superintendent of the Royal Navy Dockyard. British military planners envisioned that only a house constructed on its own hill distinct and separate from other military residential buildings in the vicinity would befit such a senior officer. Thus, this large residential house was built on a four-hectare land parcel, and was completed in 1939.

However, the outbreak of World War II necessitated a change of plans. Admiral Layton, Commander-in-Chief, China Station, occupied the house from 1940 to 1942 and used it as a venue for strategic military planning instead. Following the end of the war in 1945, the house reverted to be the official residence of the Commodore Superintendent commanding Sembawang Naval Docks, and it was officially named Nelson House, in honour of British Admiral Nelson who defeated French Emperor Napoleon at Waterloo.

In the post-war period, some 13 senior naval officers with appointments of Commander-in-Chief of British Fleet, Commander-in-Chief and Commander of Far East Fleet resided in this house. In 1958, the house was renamed Admiralty House upon its designation as the official residence of the British Royal Navy Commander-in-Chief, Far East Station. Between 1971 and 1974, the building was renamed Anzuk House and was occupied by an Admiral and an Air Vice-Marshall.

Following the Royal Navy's withdrawal in 1975, the house became State Property, and it was converted into a recreational club for Sembawang Shipyard. Since the 1990s, this house has been leased to a succession of operators as a recreational club. It was known as Yishun Country Club and Karimun Admiralty Country Club.

Old Admiralty House was gazetted as a National Monument in 2002. The restored building is currently leased to the YESS Group.

Architectural Features

This 70-year-old building is designed in the Arts and Crafts architectural style. The main structure comprises a two-storey house while a secondary structure consisting of a single-storey wing is located on the northwest corner. The former has a high hipped roof and is clad with terracotta tiles in a French pattern. Exposed fair-faced brickwork with white joints characterises the second storey's architectural design.

Old Admiralty House is widely believed to be designed by the famous British architect Edwin Lutyens. This impression is reinforced by a brass plaque within the house that states that Lutyens was the architect. However, independent research suggests no evidence that Lutyens had designed the house as he had never visited Singapore. Furthermore, there is no mention within the list of Lutyens' work that includes a house for the Royal Navy in Singapore. It is highly likely that the designer of this house was inspired by other works of Lutyens in the 1920s and 1930s, and Lutyens himself was not behind it. Nevertheless, the Old Admiralty House remains one of the most magnificent military residential buildings in Singapore.

Old Admiralty House
345 Old Nelson Road
S(758692)

OLD FORD FACTORY

Located in this northwestern part of the island is an Art Deco building that marked a turning point in the Pacific War of World War II. The Ford Factory was the site of the signing of the unconditional surrender of British and Allied forces by Lieutenant General A.E. Percival to the Imperial Japanese Army Lieutenant General Yamashita on 15 February 1942.

The Japanese forces had successfully occupied the northern and southwestern sections of Singapore island, and was poised to enter into the urban section of Singapore town in the southern section. They had seized food, fuel and ammunition dumps of the British as well as water supplies at MacRitchie Reservoir. Faced with such bleak circumstances, Percival's military staff advised that it was not possible to achieve success in a counter-attack to recapture MacRitchie Reservoir and the supplies depots in Bukit Timah. Hence, the unanimous decision was to surrender to the Japanese and to spare the civilian populace the horrors of urban warfare.

It was along the curved road that General Percival and the British delegation marched up to the factory to meet and negotiate with General Yamashita on the surrender. The surrender document was signed at the Ford Factory Board Room, and marked a break in 123 years of continuous British rule and the start of three-and-a-half years of the Japanese Occupation of Singapore and Malaya.

This building was designed by Emile Brizay, a French structural engineer, and it was constructed in 1941 for the American multi-national corporation Ford Motor Works as the first motor car assembly plant in Southeast Asia. Ford commenced operations in Singapore in 1926 at a factory located at Anson Road. It moved to its new expanded premises in late 1941, but came under Japanese control merely four months later. During the war, it was pressed into Japanese war service to produce vehicles for the Japanese military.

In post-war Singapore, this factory continued to assemble cars until 1980. Thereafter, the factory was converted into a tyre factory for Bridgestone. The property was later acquired by the Hong Leong Group in 1983. Recognising the historical legacy of this building, the

Hong Leong Group donated part of the property to the Government of Singapore in the 1990s. The front section of the building (which contains the old Board Room), along with the historical driveway, were identified for preservation and retention by the Preservation of Monuments Board. The back section of the old factory was subsequently demolished for redevelopment as a condominium.

The property was allotted to the National Heritage Board for restoration and adaptive re-use as a World War II interpretative centre. Named 'Memories at Old Ford Factory', it features a chronology of events in the Pacific War that led to the fall of Singapore and the ensuing Japanese Occupation. On display is the replicated Board Room where the surrender event took place, and a vegetable garden plot that exhibits the food crops grown by local families as part of the Japanese "Grow More Food" campaign in response to wartime food shortages. (The original table and furniture of the Board Room was requisitioned by the Australian military forces that relieved Singapore following the unconditional Japanese surrender in September 1945. The Australians shipped the items to Australia, where they are on display at the Australian War Museum in Canberra.)

The Old Ford Factory was gazetted as a National Monument in 2006 by the Preservation of Monuments Board.

Old Ford Factory

315 Upper Bukit
Timah Road
S(588192)

RAFFLES COLLEGE CAMPUS
(NUS BUKIT TIMAH CAMPUS)

Nestled away along Bukit Timah Road is the Bukit Timah campus of the National University of Singapore (NUS). While most people would associate it with being the former campus of the National Institute of Education (NIE) and the Singapore Management University (SMU), this campus has historical beginnings that go back to 1918.

A committee, headed by Sir George Maxwell, was appointed by the Straits Government in 1918 to advise on a scheme to celebrate the centenary of Singapore. The committee recommended that the advancement of education would be the most suitable memorial, and this resulted in the establishment of the Raffles College as a college for higher education. In 1919, the government set up an endowment fund for Raffles College, providing $2 million and land for the campus. The fund also received generous donations from leading local philanthropists Sir Manasseh Meyer, Oei Tiong Ham, Tan Soo Guan and Eu Tong Sen.

Legislation for the incorporation of Raffles College was passed in 1922. Following a British empire-wide architectural design competition, the design submitted by Cyril A. Farey and Graham R. Dawbarn of London was chosen as the winning entry.

Farey and Dawbarn's design envisioned the campus to consist ultimately of buildings enclosing two large quadrangles, with wings spreading out on either side of the lower quadrangle. However, the design was only implemented with the following buildings completed in 1930: an administration block with the Oei Tiong Ham Hall, lecture rooms and offices; the Manasseh Meyer Science School with four laboratories and four lecture rooms; the Eu Tong Sen Hall of Residence for 60 students; quarters for the President, four professors and three lecturers; and a 10-acre (40,470 sqm) playing field.

Raffles College opened informally for instruction on 1 June 1928 with 43 students, while its official opening by then-Governor Sir Hugh Clifford was held on 22 July 1929. When Singapore fell to Japan in World War II, the college was used as the Japanese army's headquarters. During this period, a new wing was added, which later became known

Former Raffles
College

Bukit Timah Road

as Block A (Arts Block). After the Japanese Occupation ended, Raffles College re-opened its doors in October 1946.

In 1947, a Commission on Education in Malaya, headed by Sir Alexander Carr-Saunders, concluded that both Raffles College and the King Edward VII College of Medicine could be merged to create a university. A bill creating the new University of Malaya was hence passed in the legislatures of Singapore and the Federation of Malaya on 31 March and 21 April 1949 respectively. The University of Malaya was founded on 8 October 1949 with a historic ceremony at Oei Tiong Ham Hall. With this merger, new faculties of law and engineering were added to the existing faculties of arts, science and medicine.

By 1959 though, owing to a rapid increase in demand for tertiary education in Singapore and the Malay Peninsula, the University of Malaya could no longer serve the needs of its students effectively. On 1 January 1962, a Kuala Lumpur campus was set up, while the Singapore division of the university remained in the old Raffles College campus. It was later re-designated as the University of Singapore. During this period, the Singapore campus was expanded, with the addition of a library building and a science tower.

When the University of Singapore moved to Kent Ridge in 1977, the Bukit Timah campus was used by the NIE as a teacher's college, until its relocation to Nanyang Technological University in 2001. Between August 2001 and May 2005, the SMU occupied the campus.

Since August 2006, the campus has been home to the NUS Faculty of Law, Lee Kuan Yew School of Public Policy, East Asian Institute, Institute of South Asian Studies and Asian Research Institute. The old Arts Block was also renamed Li Ka Shing Building in recent years.

With the restoration of its campus buildings, the former Raffles College was shortlisted by UNESCO as a Singapore finalist for the 2008 UNESCO Asia-Pacific Heritage Building Conservation award.

RAMAKRISHNA MISSION TEMPLE AND BOYS HOME

The Ramakrishna Mission Temple has been a familiar sight along Bartley Road for over 55 years. Flanking this three-pointed dome building are the Ramakrishna Boys Home and the Vivekananda Cultural Memorial Building.

Collectively, these structures make up the Ramakrishna Mission—a religious and charitable organisation. These represent the fruition of Sri Ramakrishna Paramahamsa and his disciple Swami Vivekananda's visions of religious harmony and service to serve fellow men. The Ramakrishna Mission was founded in India on 5 May 1897 by Swami Vivekananda to provide relief to victims of famine and plague. Centres of the Mission spread and were opened overseas by the spiritual followers of Sri Ramakrishna. Swami Vivekananda visited Singapore in 1893 and sowed the seeds of the Hindu spiritual renaissance here.

The Singapore branch of the Mission was set up on 7 August 1928. Pre-World War II, the Mission devoted itself to relief work for the poor, conducting religious and moral classes, running schools for children of Indian immigrants, and night classes. The Pacific War and Japanese invasion of Singapore caused many children to become orphans overnight. The Mission set up a temporary boys home in 1943 to care for these boys and to provide them with a formal, and moral, education.

The boys home was set up on a piece of five-acre land purchased in 1941. Within wartime Syonan, the Mission's work received humanitarian support from the Indian Independence League (IIL) led by Subash Chandra Bose. The IIL financed the construction of the first wooden dormitory building, and the home was officially opened on 14 April 1943 by Mr Mamoru Shinozaki.

After the war, the Mission decided to construct a permanent boys home. Receiving support from the greater society, work commenced on 10 December 1948 following the laying of the foundation stone by Malcolm MacDonald, Commissioner General for Southeast Asia.

Two years later, the ground floor of the new building was declared open by Jawaharlal Nehru, Prime Minister of India. The second floor was later added.

Evangelical activities continued to be organised and conducted by the Mission. The existing facilities of the Mission could not cope with an increase in the participation by the public. This required the construction of a new temple building at the Bartley Road site. Mr P Govindasamy undertook the entire financial commitment to build the temple, and he officiated at the opening ceremony in 1952.

The two-storey blue-and-white temple is one of the few Singapore buildings that exhibit Mughal characteristics with modern influences. Mughal architectural features on this building include the *Jharokha* (balcony), *Chhatri* (dome-shaped pavilions), *Chhajja* (projecting eaves supported on large carved brackets) and the *Jali* (a latticed screen with an ornamental pattern) as seen on the three arched openings on the second storey. The link to Hindu principles is evident with the symbol "Aum" present on the middle of the roof. Western influences are visibly reflected with the absence of decorative elements, as well as the presence of the large car porch and rectangular windows.

The Ramakrishna Mission Temple and Boys Home
179 Bartley Road
S(539784)

Next to the temple is the Vivekananda Cultural Memorial Building. Officially opened in 1969 by Minister for Foreign Affairs and Labour Mr S. Rajaratnam, the building became the central venue for the Mission's spiritual and cultural activities.

Today, the Ramakrishna Mission continues to conduct charitable and educational activities, and to play an important role in meeting the demands for spiritual and cultural activities within the Singapore Indian community.

ST ANDREW'S SCHOOL

Founded in 1862, St Andrew's School is the oldest Anglican school in Singapore. It has been sited in the district of Potong Pasir since making its move from Stamford Road in 1940, under the leadership of Canon R.K.S. Adams. St Andrew's School has since expanded its presence to encompass St Andrew's village, which comprises the school, chapel, Anglican Diocesan offices and three affiliated churches.

St Andrew's School is an iconic Singapore building that many alumni identify with. Designed by Frank Brewer, it has a façade featuring signature fish-scale textured trucco walls painted pink. A quadrangle is located within the school compound.

After six decades of use since 1940, the building's condition had deteriorated, and restoration work was planned for this gazetted conservation building. Work began in 2002, and was completed in 2005. The restoration process involved the repairing of the roof, re-using the original roof tiles, retaining the original architectural

St Andrew's School

55 Potong Pasir Avenue 1 S(358389)

features of the building (such as the fish-scale trucco walls, the pitched roof and large overhang), as well as keeping its original paint colour.

The restored building has won the 2006 URA Architectural Heritage Award and received an Honorable Mention in the 2007 UNESCO Asia-Pacific Heritage Awards. It has also undergone adaptive re-use for a new role as the Chapel of Resurrection.

SIONG LIM TEMPLE

Situated between the housing estate of Toa Payoh and the Pan Island Expressway (PIE), Siong Lim Temple (also known as *Lian Shan Shuang Lin Shi*) was constructed in 1912. Modelled after a famous Buddhist *cong lin* temple—*Xi Chan Si*—in Fuzhou, China, Siong Lim Temple was founded by Low Kim Pong.

Lore has it that in 1898, Low received a vision in his sleep, in which a golden light emanated from the west. The next morning, he learned that his son had a similar dream. Interpreting this as an omen, both of them went to the harbour and waited. Towards the end of the day, a group of 12 Chinese Buddhist monks and nuns arrived from India (in the western direction). Having completed a six-year pilgrimage, they were on a journey back to China. Low concluded that the vision was a call to advance Buddhism. He then decided to build a Buddhist monastery, and persuaded the monks and nuns to stay in Singapore.

Low embarked on the building of the temple between 1902 and 1908 on a 12-acre (48,600 sqm) plot of land that he had purchased in 1885. At a cost of half a million Straits Settlement dollars, the temple's rear hall (Dharma Hall), main temple (Da Xiong Bao Dian) and front hall (Tian Wang Dian), along with two towers, were constructed.

Gazetted as a National Monument in 1980, the temple underwent major restoration in 1991. The $40-million project was completed in 2002, which saw the front hall, drum hall, bell tower and main temple restored.

Siong Lim Temple
184€ Jalan Toa Payoh
S(319941)

SUN YAT SEN NANYANG MEMORIAL HALL

The Sun Yat Sen Nanyang Memorial Hall is a Community Heritage Institution managed by the National Heritage Board and the Singapore Chinese Chamber of Commerce Foundation. This museum honours Dr Sun Yat Sen (1866–1925) as the Father of modern China, and tells the story of the Singapore Chinese community and its position within the Chinese Diaspora in supporting Dr Sun's revolutionary work.

Constructed in 1900, this two-storey building was purchased by Singapore rubber magnate Teo Eng Hock for his mother's use. Teo subsequently offered the use of the premises, named *Wan Qing Yuan*, to Dr Sun on his third visit to Singapore in 1906 as the local branch of the *Tongmenhui*. Dr Sun resided here on his subsequent visits. This building was Dr Sun's base, from which it reached out to supporters within the Chinese communities in the Malay Peninsula, Thailand, Indo-China and Dutch East Indies (present-day Indonesia) to raise funds for armed uprisings to overthrow the Qing Dynasty. Eventually, a successful uprising culminated in the Chinese Revolution of 1911.

In 1937, about a decade after Dr Sun's death, the building was purchased by local supporters of Dr Sun, and donated to the Chinese Republican Government with the intention of retaining it as a monument to him. The Singapore Chinese Chamber of Commerce & Industry (SCCCI) was made custodian of the property. During the Japanese Occupation, this building was requisitioned and occupied by the Imperial Japanese Army. After the war, the building housed the Singapore branch of the *Kuomintang*, and in 1951, was passed back to the SCCCI. Subsequently, the SCCCI sought to convert the Sun Yat Sen Villa into a museum. The museum was officially opened in 1966, in conjunction with the commemorative activities honouring the centenary of Dr Sun's birth.

Gazetted as a National Monument in 1994, the building has since undergone various rounds of restoration. In 2001, this monument was renamed the Sun Yat Sen Nanyang Memorial Hall by the SCCCI. Permanent exhibits on display include bronze statues of Chinese revolutionaries, paintings, historical photos and artefacts, as well as film clips documenting Dr Sun's work.

Sun Yat Sen
Nanyang
Memorial Hall

12 Tai Gin Road
S(327874)

晚晴園

此古蹟原名"明珍廬"，為殷商宅居，后為張永福買下，供母養老，易名為"晚晴園"。

清末孫中山先生奔走革命，一九零五年來到新加坡，一九零六年組織中國同盟會南洋支部，孫中山先生在此借住，并用作舉會活動場所。

辛亥革命成功之後，晚晴園人去樓空，荒蕪剩澤，破損不堪。

一九三七年，李光前、李儁承、陳延謙、周獻瑞、李振殿和楊吉兆等六位先賢捐資買回晚晴園，獻給中國政府，經修葺並充實文物，恢復舊觀後，定名為"孫逸仙別墅"。

一九四二年日本占領時期，晚晴園文物再度蕩然無存，屋身宗壞傾頹塌，一九四六年，中華民國政府開晚晴園用作國民黨支部公署，一九五九年，英國陸各地政府廢除此園民黨在新加坡活動，民國政府遂義房產所有權移交新加坡中華總商會，一九六四年，總商會轉榮教修葺，並于一九六六年將孫先生歷史文物圖陳日始將藏死難人員遺物縣列於此，供大眾瞻仰參觀。

一九九四年晚晴園被列為國家古蹟，一九九七年總商會決議翻新修建晚晴園，如郭整修添文物，正式命名為"孫中山南洋紀念館"，此項工程歷時四年餘，二零零一年九月完工，十一月十二日由李光耀資政主持開幕。

SUNGEI BULOH WETLANDS RESERVE

Formerly utilised for fish and prawn farming, Sungei Buloh was chanced upon by a group of bird-watchers from the then Malayan Nature Society (Singapore Branch) and identified as a site of significant ecological integrity. Following visits by top government officials, it was then opened as Sungei Buloh Nature Park in 1993, under the jurisdiction of the National Parks Board. Throughout the years, facilities were constructed to enable greater public access to the 130-hectare park; outreach and education programmes were started, and projects supporting biodiversity conservation and research were initiated. In recognition of the role that Sungei Buloh played in nature conservation, it was gazetted as a nature reserve (and hence renamed Sungei Buloh Wetland Reserve) in 2002, one of four such reserves in Singapore. It gained prominence on the international stage when it was accepted into the East Asian Australasian Shorebird Site Network in the same year, and was marked as Singapore's first ASEAN Heritage Park in 2003.

With more than 220 recorded bird species, close to 20 mammal species, 45 reptile and amphibian, 100 fish and 50 butterfly species, it is clear how Sungei Buloh lives up to its status as a nature reserve. Scores of migratory birds of all shapes and sizes descend upon the mudflats in their hundreds during the annual migratory season from September to March. There are uncountable species of weird and colourful insects, many of which remain waiting to be discovered. Schools of fish swim in the brackish waters, and even estuarine crocodiles and otters can be spotted lazing in the sun or splashing around catching fish. At high tide, tree-climbing crabs refine the concept of getting

close to nature as they crawl up tree trunks and boardwalk railings, almost within reach of a toddler's hand. At low tide, mudskippers can be seen exposed on the mud banks, along with horseshoe crabs navigating their way through narrow streams.

There is, however, no guarantee that a visitor to Sungei Buloh would see all

these things. Many wild animals are wary of large moving objects or loud sounds such as those originating from large family groups or overly-excited school groups. One has to move about quietly and observantly—"You look with your ears"—for very often, an animal is heard before it is seen.

A number of outreach activities are held regularly at Sungei Buloh. Photo and poster exhibitions, mangrove reforestation, coastal clean-ups, drawing lessons and photography courses are routine events. There is also a team of experienced volunteer nature guides who impart their passion and transform people's visits from a tour into an experience.

Sungei Buloh is where mangroves and wetland wildlife thrive. So too thrives the human spirit. A visit to the reserve can be more inspirational than informative, and it will proudly play its role in developing a sense of responsibility and concern for the natural environment in our youth for many more years to come.

Sungei Buloh
Wetlands Reserve

301 Neo Tiew
Crescent, S(718925)

TOMB OF LIM BO SENG

First-time visitors to the MacRitchie Reservoir may find it strange to see a Chinese tomb located within the reservoir grounds. However, this is no ordinary tomb, but that of Mr Lim Bo Seng—Singapore's most well-known martyr and military hero of World War II.

After the fall of Singapore in February 1942, Lim Bo Seng left for British India. While in Calcutta, he met Major John Davis and Captain Richard Broome, who were recruiting men to form an anti-Japanese resistance force. Lim joined the Indian Mission of Special Operations Executive (later designated as Force 136) and underwent military training to become an agent. This unit was deployed to perform acts of sabotage and espionage against the Japanese in the Malay Peninsula.

Lim and his men slipped back into Malaya by submarine in 1943. He was amongst the Force 136 agents who returned to wage anti-Japanese activities, while laying groundwork for a planned Allied invasion of Malaya. However, Lim was captured by the Japanese during an intelligence-gathering operation in Ipoh in March 1944. He died from serious injuries sustained from Japanese interrogation and torture, and was buried in Malaya's Batu Gajah prison.

Following the war, Lim's remains were exhumed and returned for burial in Singapore. He was accorded a funeral with full military honours, and was buried on the grounds of MacRitchie Reservoir on 13 January 1946. Memorial services were held in Ipoh, Kuala Lumpur and Singapore. Lim was also posthumously promoted to the rank of Army Major-General by Generalissimo Chiang Kai-Shek of the Republic of China.

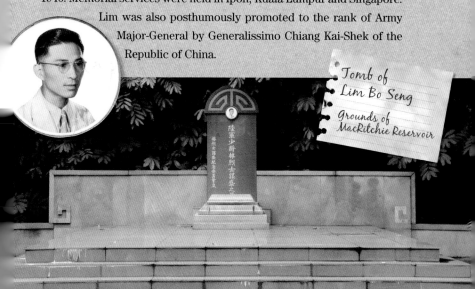

Tomb of
Lim Bo Seng

Grounds of
MacRitchie Reservoir

GLOSSARY OF ARCHITECTURAL TERMS

Art Deco: The term Art Deco was coined from the Exposition des Arts Decoratifs held in Paris in 1925. It is a geometric design style that began as a reaction to the Art Nouveau style which had declined in the early 20th century.

Arts and Crafts: A late-19th century movement to revive handicrafts, Arts and Crafts architecture sought a spiritual connection with the surrounding environment, both natural and manmade. The movement began primarily as a search for authentic and meaningful styles for the 19th century and as a reaction to the Industrial Revolution.

balustrade: A series of short pillars that support a rail.

bas relief: A low relief carving that protrudes slightly from the background.

basilica: Refers to early Christian churches with a nave and two or more aisles.

belfry: The upper storey of a tower in which one or more bells are hung.

buttresses: A mass of stonework / brickwork built against (or projecting from) a wall to give it additional strength.

capital: The top section of a column.

Cenotaph: A monument to one or more persons who are buried elsewhere.

cinquefoil: A prefix indicating the number of foils between cusps (projecting points) in Gothic window tracery. Cinquefoil indicates five foils.

Classical Renaissance: It refers to architecture of the period between the early-15th and 17th centuries in different regions of Europe, during which there was a conscious revival and development of certain elements of Greek and Roman thought and material culture.

corbels: A projecting bracket that supports a beam.

Corinthian: An order in classical architecture invented by the Greeks in the 5th century BCE.

cupola: A dome on a drum surmounted by a lantern.

Doric: A classical architecture order that is divided into Greek Doric and Roman Doric. The former has fluted columns, no base, and a capital with simple molding and an abacus. The latter column is slimmer and non-fluted, and has a low base with smaller capital.

eaves: The lower edge of a sloping roof.

fanlights: A window over a door. It is often semi-circular in shape.

finial: An ornament with a leafy pattern on top of a pinnacle, gable, spire or canopy.

French Renaissance: A style of architecture imported from Italy during the early 16th century and developed in the light of local French architectural traditions.

fretwork: Decorative geometrical carvings or metalwork.

gopuram: A large towered gateway at the entrance of an Indian Hindu temple.

Ionic: An order in classical architecture that originated in Asia Minor in the 6th century BCE. It has a character of scroll-shaped volutes on the column's capital, dentils in the cornice and a frieze that may bear continuous low-relief decoration.

Italian Renaissance: A style of architecture that emerged in Italy in the 15th century which saw the use of classical motifs and the architectural orders of antiquity.

Jian nian: *Jian nian* means "cut and paste". It is a craft popular with the Southern Chinese. *Jian nian* involves gluing colourful porcelain shards to create decorative—and often three-dimensional—motifs. The traditional method involves the use of coloured ceramic shards (pottery bowls specially fabricated and broken with pliers) by Chinese artisans to paste the shards to form decorative displays on the roofs of traditional Chinese buildings. This method is used by the Hokkien and Teochew people.

keramat: This Malay word is derived from the Arabic term "karamah", which refers specifically to the *wali* (plural *waliya* in Arabic), a close friend of God (Allah), or a pious person. It may be applied to the living saint (sheikh), but is also applied to the dead.

minaret: A tall tower with projecting balconies connected to a mosque. It is used to call the people to prayer.

moldings: A sculpted band with a distinctive profile that is used to decorate a range of protruding surfaces. These include column bases, capitals, door and window jambs, and the edges of panels.

Mughal: Mughal architecture, an amalgamation of Islamic, Persian and Indian architecture, is the style developed by the Mughal empire during the 16th and 17th centuries in the Indian subcontinent. It is seen in present-day India, Pakistan and Bangladesh.

Neo-Byzantine: An architectural revival style, most frequently seen in religious, institutional and public buildings. It incorporates elements of the Byzantine style associated with Eastern and Orthodox Christian architecture dating from the 5th to 11th centuries.

Neoclassical Palladin: See Palladian.

Neo-Georgian: An architecture style that emulates features and details of Georgian architecture, including a symmetrical façade, but is commonly historically inaccurate. Found primarily in buildings constructed in the 19th and 20th centuries.

Neo-Gothic: An architectural style emerging from an architectural movement of the Victorian era that sought to revive medieval form as distinct from the prevalent classical style of the era. This was seen in the Gothic revival within architecture of the period.

Neo-Renaissance: An all-encompassing term used to refer to the 19th century architectural revival styles that were neither Greek nor Gothic, but which instead drew inspiration from a wide range of classicizing Italian modes.

obelisk: A tall stone shaft. Usually cut from a single stone and tapering at the summit, it is a feature of ancient Egyptian architecture.

Palladian: A style of building based on the work of 16th century Italian architect Andrea Palladio. The style followed classical Roman conventions and was popular in England during the 18th century.

parapet: A low wall running the length of any feature, such as a balcony, terrace, or bridge, immediately below which is a sudden drop.

pediment: A low-pitched gable end of a building, usually above a portico. A distinctive feature of classical and classically inspired architecture.

pilaster: A shallow pier that stands out slightly from a wall and in classical buildings. It has the features of one of the orders.

portico: An open space with a roof supported by columns, at the entrance of a building.

quadrangle: A rectangular courtyard found on buildings with all four sides.

rose window: A large circular window with tracery arranged like the spokes of a wheel. It is often seen on Gothic buildings.

rotunda: A circular building or room with a dome.

spire: A tall slender structure that tapers to a point and rises from a tower or roof.

steeple: A tower with a spire on top.

stela: An upright stone slab adorned with an inscription and sometimes a figure. It is used to mark a grave or as a commemorative structure. Usually found on the wall of a building.

trusses: A structure comprising one or more triangular units constructed with straight slender members whose ends are connected at joints referred to as nodes.

turret: A small tower that projects from the corner of a building or wall.

tympanum: The triangular space enclosed by the moldings of a pediment. It is also the delineated space between the lintel of a door and the arch situated above it.

TRANSPORT INFORMATION

Name	Location	Buses	MRT
Abdul Gaffoor Mosque	41 Dunlop St	2N, 4N, 48, 56, 57, 131, 166, 170, 851, 960, 980	Little India (NE7)
Alsagoff Arab School	Jalan Sultan	107, 107M	Lavender (EW11)
Anderson Bridge	Singapore River	75, 100, 107, 130, 131, 167	Raffles Place (EW14 / NS26)
Armenian Church	Armenian St / Hill St	2, 12, 32, 33, 51, 61, 63, 80, 197	City Hall (EW13 / NS25)
Baba House	Neil Rd	61, 166, 167, 196, 197	Outram (EW16 / NE3)
Bidadari Memorial Garden	Off Mount Vernon Rd (Near to Gurkha Camp)	100, 135, 155	Kovan (NE13)
Bukit Timah Hill & Nature Reserve	Hindhede Rd (Off Upp Bukit Timah Rd)	67, 75, 170, 171, 179, 184, 852, 961, 961C	None
Cathedral of Good Shepherd	Junction of Queen's St/ Bras Basah Rd	130, 133, 145, 197, 851, 960	City Hall (EW13 / NS25)
Cavenagh Bridge	North Bridge Rd / South Bridge Rd	1N, 2N, 3N, 4N, 5N, 6N, 61, 124, 145, 166, 174, 174e, 197	Raffles Place (EW14 / NS26)
Cenotaph	Connaught Dr	75, 100, 107, 130, 131, 167	City Hall (EW13 / NS25)
Chesed-El Synagogue	Oxley Rise	7, 14, 14e, 16, 36, 65, 77, 106, 111, 123, 124, 128, 143, 162M, 162, 167, 171, 174, 174e, 175, 190, 502A, 502, 700A, 700	Dhoby Ghaut (NS24 / NE6)
CHIJMES	30 Victoria St	130, 133, 145, 197, 851, 960	City Hall (EW13 / NS25)
Chinese High School Clock Tower	Bukit Timah Rd	66, 67, 74, 151, 154, 156, 157, 170, 171, 174, 852, 961, 961C	Newton (NS21)
Church of Nativity of the Blessed Virgin Mary	Near junction of Upp Serangoon Rd/Hougang Ave 8	51, 72, 80, 101, 119, 136, 153	Hougang (NE14)
Church of Our Lady of Lourdes	50 Ophir Rd	2N, 4N, 48, 57, 130, 851, 960	Bugis (EW12)
Church of Sacred Heart	Junction of Tank Rd/ Clemenceau Ave	64, 123, 139, 143	Dhoby Ghaut (NS24 / NE6)

Name	Location	Buses	MRT
Church of Sts Peter & Paul	Queen's St	7, 14, 14e, 16, 36, 77, 106, 111, 128, 131, 162, 162M, 167, 171, 175, 502A, 502, 518A, 518, 578, 579, 581, 587, 590, 598, 700, 700A, 857	City Hall (EW13 / NS25)
Church of St Teresa	Junction of Kampong Bahru Rd/ Bukit Purmei	61, 124, 143, 166	HarbourFront (NE1) / Outram (EW16 / NE3)
Civilian War Memorial	Junction of Beach Rd/ Stamford Rd	14, 14e, 16, 36, 77, 106, 111, 128, 130, 131, 133, 162M, 162, 167, 171, 502, 502A, 518, 518A, 578, 579, 581, 700A, 700, 857, 960	City Hall (EW13 / NS25)
Clifford Pier	Collyer Quay	10, 10e, 57, 70, 75, 97e, 97, 100, 107, 128, 130, 131, 162, 167, 196e, 531, 546, 587, 590, 597, 598, 700	Raffles Place (EW14 / NS26)
Coleman Bridge	New Bridge Rd	2, 12, 33, 54, 63, 124, 143, 147, 190, 851, 961, 961C, 970, CT18, CT8	Clark Quay (NE5)
Command House	Kheam Hock Rd	48, 66, 67, 151, 153, 154, 156, 170, 171, 186	Newton (NS21)
Dalhousie Obelisk	Empress Place	75, 100, 107, 130, 131, 167	Raffles Place (EW14 / NS26)
Elgin Bridge	Singapore River	75, 100, 107, 130, 131, 167	Raffles Place (EW14 / NS26)
Empress Place Building (Asian Civilisation Musm)	Empress Place	75, 100, 107, 130, 131, 167	Raffles Place (EW14 / NS26)
Family Court Building	Havelock Rd	1N, 2N, 3N, 4N, 5N, 6N, 51, 64, 123, 186	Clark Quay (NE5)
Fook Tet Soo Khek Temple	Palmer Rd	70, 75, 107, 128, 130, 162, 167, 186, 196, 196e, 400, 402, 530, 531, 546, 587, 588, 590, 597, 598, 599, 700, 970	Tanjong Pagar (EW15)
Former Attorney General's Chambers	High St	75, 100, 107, 130, 131, 167	Raffles Place (EW14 / NS26)
Former Hill Street Police Station (MICA Building)	Junction of Hill St/River Valley Rd	124, 145, 147, 166, 174, 174e, 190, 851	City Hall (EW13 / NS25)
Former Istana of Sultan of Singapore (Malay Heritage Centre)	Junction of Sultan Gate/Pahang St	7, 32, 51, 61, 63, 80, 145, 175, 197	Bugis (EW12)

Name	Location	Buses	MRT
Former St. Joseph's Inst (Singapore Art Museum)	Junction of Bras Basah Rd/Waterloo St	7, 14, 14e, 16, 36, 77, 106, 111, 128, 131, 162, 162M, 167, 171, 175, 502A, 502, 518, 518A, 578, 579, 581, 587, 590, 598, 700, 700A	City Hall (EW13 / NS25) / Dhoby Ghaut (NS24 / NE6)
Former Tao Nan School (Peranakan Museum)	Armenian St	2, 12, 32, 33, 51, 61, 63, 80, 197	City Hall (EW13 / NS25)
Fort Canning Hill	Canning Rise	2, 12, 32, 33, 51, 61, 63, 80, 197	City Hall (EW13 / NS25)
Goodwood Park Hotel	Scotts Rd	5, 54, 105, 124, 128, 132, 143, 162M, 162, 167, 171, 190, 518A, 518, 578, 579, 581, 587, 590, 598, 700, 700A	Orchard (NS22)
Hajjah Fatimah Mosque	Beach Rd	100	Lavender (EW11)
Hill Street Fire Station	Hill St	124, 145, 147, 166, 174, 174e, 190, 851	City Hall (EW13 / NS25)
House of Tan Yoke Nee	Penang Rd	7, 14, 14e, 16, 36, 65, 77, 106, 111, 123, 124, 128, 143, 162M, 162, 167, 171, 174, 174e, 175, 190, 502A, 502, 700A, 700	Dhoby Ghaut (NS24 / NE6)
Indian National Army Memorial Historic Marker	Connaught Dr	75, 100, 107, 130, 131, 167	City Hall (EW13 / NS25)
Istana & Sri Temasek	Orchard Rd	1N, 2N, 3N, 4N, 5N, 6N, 7, 14e, 14, 16, 36, 77, 106, 111, 124, 128, 162, 162M, 167, 171, 174, 174e, 175, 190, 502, 502A, 518, 518A, 700, 700A,	Dhoby Ghaut (NS24 / NE6)
Jamae Mosque	South Bridge Rd	61, 166, 197	Tanjong Pagar (EW15)
Japanese Cemetery	Chuan Hoe Ave (off Yio Chu Kang Rd)	43, 70, 70M, 76, 103, 103M, 109, 147, 156, 534	Yio Chu Kang (NS15) / Hougang NE14
Jinrikisha Station	Junction of Neil Rd/Maxwell Rd	80, 145	Dhoby Ghaut (NS24 / NE6)
Kampong Kapor Methodist Church	Junction of Kampong Kapor Rd/Veerasamy Rd	23, 64, 65, 66, 67, 130, 139, 147, 857	Little India (NE7)
Keppel Railway Station	Keppel Rd	10, 30, 57, 80, 97, 97e, 100, 131, 145	Tanjong Pagar (EW15)
Keramat Habib Noh	Palmer Rd	70, 75, 107, 128, 130, 162, 167, 186, 196, 196e, 400, 402, 530, 531, 546, 587, 588, 590, 597, 598, 599, 700, 970	Tanjong Pagar (EW15)
Kranji War Cemetery	Woodlands Rd	160, 170, 178, 960, 961, 961C	Kranji (NS7)

Name	Location	Buses	MRT
Labrador Park	End of Labrador Villa Rd	408	HarbourFront (NE1)
Lau Pa Sat (Old Telok Ayer Market)	Junction of Robinson Rd/Cross St	10e, 10, 196, 196e, 531, 532, 533, 534, 535, 536, 538, 539, 542, 543, 544, 545, 548, 549, 550, 552, 553, 554, 555, 556, 557, 558, 559, 560, 561, 563, 564, 565, 566, 569, 585	Raffles Place (EW14 / NS26) / Tanjong Pagar
Lim Bo Seng Memorial	Connaught Dr	107	City Hall (EW13 / NS25)
MacDonald House	Orchard Rd	1N, 2N, 3N, 4N, 5N, 6N, 7, 14e, 14, 16, 36, 77, 106, 111, 124, 128, 162, 162M, 167, 171, 174, 174e, 175, 190, 502, 502A, 518, 518A, 700, 700A	Dhoby Ghaut (NS24 / NE6)
Maghain Aboth Synagogue	Waterloo St	7, 14, 14e, 16, 36, 77, 106, 111, 128, 131, 162, 162M, 167, 171, 175, 502A, 502, 518, 518A, 578, 579, 581, 587, 590, 598, 700, 700A	City Hall (EW13 / NS25)
Malabar Mosque	Junction of Victoria St/ Jalan Sultan	2, 7, 12, 32, 33, 51, 61, 63, 80, 107, 107M, 133, 145, 175, 197, NR7	Lavender (EW11)
Masonic Lodge	23A Coleman St	2, 12, 32, 33, 51, 61, 63, 80, 197	City Hall (EW13 / NS25)
Middle Road Church (Sculpture Square)	Junction of Waterloo St/ Middle Rd	56	Bugis (EW12)/ Dhoby Ghaut (NS24 / NE6)
Monument to the Early Founders of Singapore	1 Canning Rise	2, 12, 32, 33, 51, 61, 63, 80, 197	City Hall (EW13 / NS25)
MPH Building	Stamford Rd	7, 14, 14e, 16, 36, 77, 106, 111, 124, 128, 131, 147, 162M, 162, 167, 171, 174, 174e, 175, 190, 502, 502A, 700, 700A, 857, NR7	City Hall (EW13 / NS25)
Nagore Dargah	Junction of Telok Ayer St/ Boon Tat St	10e, 10, 196, 196e, 531, 532, 533, 534, 535, 536, 538, 539, 542, 543, 544, 545, 548, 549, 550, 552, 553, 554, 555, 556, 557, 558, 559, 560, 561, 563, 564, 565, 566, 569, 585	Tanjong Pagar (EW15)
National Museum of Singapore	Stamford Rd	7, 14, 14e, 16, 36, 77, 106, 111, 124, 128, 131, 147, 162M, 162, 167, 171, 174, 174e, 175, 190, 502, 502A, 700, 700A, 857, NR7	Dhoby Ghaut (NS24 / NE6)
Old Admiralty House	Junction of Canberra Rd/ Old Nelson Rd	167, 856, 882, 980	Admiralty (NS10)

Name	Location	Buses	MRT
Old Ford Factory	Upper Bukit Timah Rd	67, 75, 170, 171, 178, 184, 961, 961C	Bukit Batok (NS2)
Old Fort Tanjong Katong	Fort Rd (Katong Park)	30, 30e, 158	Kallang (EW10)
Old Kallang Airport Tower	Stadium Link (Off Nicoll Highway)	2, 7, 12, 13, 32, 33, 51, 63, 67, 80, 100, 197	Kallang (EW10)
Old Nanyang University Archway	Yunnan Garden Park at Jurong West St 93	182, 182M, 193	Boon Lay (EW27)
Old Nanyang University (Library & Administration Building, Memorial)	50 Nanyang Ave	199	Boon Lay (EW27)
Old Parliament House (Arts House at The Old Parliament)	Empress Place	75, 100, 107, 130, 131, 167	Raffles Place (EW14 / NS26)
Old Supreme Court & City Hall	St Andrew Rd	75, 100, 107, 130, 131, 167	City Hall (EW13 / NS25)
Old Thong Chai Medical Institution	Junction of Eu Tong Sen St/ Merchant Rd	2, 12, 33, 51, 61, 63, 80, 174e, 174, 197, 961, 961C,	Clark Quay (NE5)
Orchard Road Presbyterian Church	Orchard Rd (next to YMCA)	7, 14e, 14, 16, 36, 64, 65, 77, 106, 111, 124, 128, 139, 162M, 162, 167, 171, 174e, 174, 175, 190, 502A, 502, 700A, 700	Dhoby Ghaut (NS24 / NE6)
Ord Bridge	Singapore River	64, 123, 139, 143, 1N, 2N, 3N, 4N, 5N, 6N, 32, 54, 195	Clark Quay (NE5)
Padang	St Andrew's Rd	75, 100, 107, 130, 131, 167	City Hall (EW13 / NS25) / Raffles Place (EW14 / NS26)
Prinsep Street Presbyterian Church	Prinsep St	1N, 2N, 3N, 4N, 5N, 6N, 64, 65, 131, 139, 147, 166, 857	Dhoby Ghaut (NS24 / NE6)
Raffles College Campus (NUS Bt Timah)	Bukit Timah Rd	48, 66, 67, 151, 153, 154, 156, 170, 171, 186	Newton (NS21)

Name	Location	Buses	MRT
Raffles Hotel	Junction of Bras Basah Rd/ Beach Rd	14, 14e, 16, 77, 106, 111, 128, 131, 133, 162M, 162, 167, 171, 502, 502A, 518, 518A, 578, 579, 581, 700A, 700, 857, 960	City Hall (EW13 / NS25)
Ramakrishna Mission	179 Bartley Rd	28, 93, 158	Bartley (CC12)
Singapore Botanical Gdns	Junction of Napier Rd / Cluny Rd	7, 75, 77, 105, 106, 123, 174e, 174,	Orchard (NS22)
Singapore General Hospital (Bowyer Block Clock Tower, College of Medicine Building, Tan Teck Guan Building)	Outram Rd	33, 63, 75, 174e, 174, 851, 970	Outram (EW16 / NE3)
Singapore Volunteer Corps (SVC) Memorial	Beach Rd (across from Raffles Hotel)	14, 14e, 16, 36, 77, 106, 111, 128, 130, 131, 133, 162M, 162, 167, 171, 502, 502A, 518, 518A, 578, 579, 581, 700A, 700, 857, 960	City Hall (EW13 / NS25)
Siong Lim Temple	Kim Keat Ave	57, 238, 535, 8, 26, 31, 90, 142, 151, 151e, 154, 966, 985	Toa Payoh (NS19)
Sri Mariamman Temple	South Bridge Rd	61, 166, 197	Tanjong Pagar (EW15)
Sri Perumal Temple	Junction of Perumal Rd/ Serangoon Rd	21, 23, 64, 65, 66, 67, 125, 130, 147, 857	Little India (NE7)
St Andrew's Cathedral	Junction of North Bridge Rd/ Stamford Rd	1N, 2N, 3N, 4N, 5N, 6N, 61, 124, 145, 166, 174, 174e, 197	City Hall (EW13 / NS25)
St Andrew's School	Graham White Dr	13, 107M, 133, 147, 853, 853C	Potong Pasir (NE10)
St George's Church	Minden Rd	7, 75, 77, 105, 106, 123, 174e, 174	Orchard (NS22)
St James Power Station	Gateway Ave	10, 30, 30e, 57, 61, 97, 97e, 100, 131, 143, 145, 166	HarbourFront (NE1)
St Joseph's Church	Victoria St	130, 133, 145, 197, 851, 960	Bugis (EW12)
Sultan Mosque	Junction of Arab St/North Bridge Rd	7, 32, 51, 61, 63, 80, 145, 175, 197	Bugis (EW12)
Sun Yat Sen Nanyang Memorial Hall	Junction of Ah Hood Rd/ Tai Gin Rd	139, 565	Toa Payoh (NS19)

Name	Location	Buses	MRT
Sungei Buloh Wetlands Reserve	Neo Tiew Crescent (off Kranji Way & Neo Tiew Rd)	925C, Kranji Express (only at Kranji MRT station)	Kranji (NS7)
Tan Kim Seng Fountain	Connaught Dr	107	City Hall (EW13 / NS25)
Telok Ayer Chinese Methodist Church	Junction of Telok Ayer St/Cecil St	57, 131, 167, 186, 700, 970	Tanjong Pagar (EW15)
Thandayuthapani Temple (Tank Road Temple)	Off junction of Clemenceau Ave/ River Valley Rd	64, 123, 139, 143	Dhoby Ghaut (NS24 / NE6)
Thian Hock Keng Temple	Telok Ayer St	10e, 10, 196, 196e, 531, 532, 533, 534, 535, 536, 538, 539, 542, 543, 544, 545, 548, 549, 550, 552, 553, 554, 555, 556, 557, 558, 559, 560, 561, 563, 564, 565, 566, 569, 585	Tanjong Pagar (EW15)
Tiong Bahru SIT Flats	Kim Tian Rd / Jalan Membina	5, 16, 33, 63, 123, 195, 851, NR5	Tiong Bahru (EW17)
Tomb of Lim Bo Seng	MacRitchie Reservoir	52, 74, 93, 157, 165, 852, 855	Toa Payoh (NS19) / Braddell (NS18); Marymount (CC16)
Tou Mu Kung Temple	Near junction of Upper Serangoon Rd/ Hillside Dr	80, 81, 82, 101, 107M, 136, 153	Kovan (NE13)
Victoria Theatre & Concert Hall	Empress Place	75, 100, 107, 130, 131, 167	Raffles Place (EW14 / NS26)
Yue Hwa Emporium	Junction of Eu Tong Sen St/ Upper Cross St	54, 124, 145, 147, 166, 190, 851	Chinatown (NE4)
Yueh Hai Ching Temple	Junction of Church St/Philip St	186, 530, 588, 599, 970, NR1, NR2, NR5, NR6, NR7, NR8	Raffles Place (EW14 / NS26)

SINGAPORE TAXIS COMPANIES

6-Dial-Cab	6342-5222	SMART Cab	6485-7777
City Cab	6552-1111	SMRT	6555-8888
Comfort	6552-1111	Trans Cab	6555-3333
Premier	6363-6888	Yellow Top	6293-5545
Prime Taxi	6778-0808		

INDEX OF PLACES

246

ABOUT THE AUTHORS

Wan Meng Hao

Hong Kong-born Meng Hao spent much of his childhood in Singapore and his late teens in Vancouver, Canada. A graduate of the University of Minnesota Twin Cities (USA) where he read Political Science and Journalism, he has an MA degree from the National University of Singapore (NUS). He has been a copywriter at McCann-Erickson as well as a Research Staff of the Department of Geography, NUS and as a Heritage Officer with the National Heritage Board. His last post was Executive Secretary of the Preservation of Monuments Board. He received training in the Management and Conservation of World Heritage Sites at the United Nations Institute of Training and Research (UNITAR) and was Singapore's Observer at the UNESCO Regional Workshop on Periodic Reporting Follow-up for North-East and South-East Asia in 2005. A life-long member of the Scout Movement, he is currently a Resource Commissioner of the Singapore Scout Association.

His past collaborative works to date include *Singapore's 100 Historic Places* (2002); *Scouting in Singapore 1910–2000* (2003); and *Malays/Muslims in Singapore: Selected readings in History, 1819–1965* (2006). He was a contributor to the *Singapore: The Encyclopedia (2006)*. This is his fourth book.

Jacqueline Lau

A hobbyist wildlife—among other things—photographer, Jacqueline has a rather confused sense of the word 'home' having been born in Hong Kong, raised in Singapore, and schooled in Sydney and London. She is fascinated by anything animal (really anything: feathered, furred, scaled or exoskeleton-ed) and has worked to arm herself with first an Ecology degree and then a masters in Environmental Technology (Business and the Environment) from Imperial College London. Her photos have frequently been provided to non-profit organisations, schools and museums, and have been used in a number of digital and print publications in Singapore and abroad. She maintains an online portfolio at photos.talfryn.com. Her other interests are politics, philosophy, history of both the natural and modern kind, and some light anthropology.

Her cross-cultural exposure has propelled her interest in social and cultural heritage, and her contributions to this book marks her first attempt to capture through the lens the places which she and many others have been taking for granted. Like any true Scout and global nomad, she is not about to stop exploring what life has to offer any time soon. Ever the dogged wanderer.

ABOUT THE PHOTOGRAPHERS

Marcus Ng

Marcus is a freelance writer and editor who dabbles in photography (www. flickr.com/photos/budak). Explorations into the natural and human heritage of Singapore and Southeast Asia occupy his waking hours, which he tries to fill with lonely walkabouts through the city's grubbier quarters and lesser known shores. He also needs no excuse for a pint and tries to (gently) poke every cat and any other small animal he encounters. These bad habits are disapproved of by Angel the cat and Tweety the budgie, who share the task of house training Marcus to ensure he is fit for civil society. They are not always successful.

Lin Yangchen

Yangchen is a biologist by training. He took up photography in 2006 for the purpose of documenting wildlife in Singapore but has since expanded his scope to action, portraiture, astronomy, aviation, architecture, landscape, photo-micrography, photojournalism, sports and travel. Besides solo exhibitions at Singapore's national library, botanic gardens and nature reserves, his photographs have been featured in *Asian Geographic* magazine and educational publications. His portfolio can be viewed at www.yangchen.smugmug.com.

Lee Tsen Yang

Tsen Yang, a self-professed 'green' urbanist, is interested in telling his side of the story through street and still life photography. His work was recently featured in a NParks publication on skyrise greenery, which is aimed at encouraging a softer, lusher built-form through roof gardens and vertical planting. He aspires to be a professional (weekend) photojournalist one day, although he is contented to being an amateur for now. Tsen Yang currently runs around with J.A.I, a four-piece band which comprises four fun-loving friends, doing gigs for community and other events.

Cai Yixiong

A naturalist in Southeast Asia. Unlike most others, Dr Cai started photography for scientific purposes as to simply record the image of various species that he has studied. However, while getting to know more about photography and more about the biodiversity of the environment, he found himself getting a great deal of fun out of playing with cameras and various lenses and accessories in the field. He has learnt to improve his skills by attending courses, practising in the field and discussing with a group of outing buddies, as well as posting photos to the website of Nature Photographic Society of Singapore for comments and critique.

Tony Png

Tony was introduced to photography as a student and has been hooked on it ever since. A lifelong hobby photographer, nature—in the manifestations of landscapes, plants, flowers, insects, etc—has been the subject of his photographic career which has seen him travelling within Southeast Asia as well as China, Europe and Australia. Tony is a Committee Member of the Nature Photographic Society (Singapore) and Photographic Society of Singapore. His photos can be viewed at www.flickr.com/photos/pngtony.

PHOTO CREDITS

Cai Yixiong: pgs 84, 107 (top), 148 (top), 150, 220-221, 226 (both), 227 (all).

Jacqueline Lau: pgs 3 (bottom), 4, 10 (both), 11, 12 (top), 16, 17 (bottom), 18, 19, 21 (both), 22, 27, 29, 31, 32, 34 (bottom), 38, 40, 41 (both), 46 (both), 47 (bottom) , 55 (bottom), 61, 62, 67, 69, 75, 89, 94, 102, 103 (both), 117, 120, 121, 122 (both), 124 (both), 125 (all), 126, 127, 128, 131 (bottom), 139, 140, 144, 145 (bottom), 153, 163, 164, 167 (middle & bottom), 186 (both), 208, 210, 211, 214, 218, 220 (inset), 222, 230, 231 (all), 232 (both), 233, back cover.

Lee Tsen Yang: pg 137 (both).

Lin Yangchen: cover, pgs 3 (top), 49, 50 (both), 63, 71, 72 (right), 82 (both), 92, 101, 129 (top), 145 (top), 155 (top), 185, 213.

Marcus Ng: pgs 34 (top), 64, 97 (main), 99, 105 (top), 109, 112, 129 (bottom), 170–171, 188–189, 197.

Tony Png: pgs 45, 51, 53, 57, 59, 60, 64, 78, 80-81, 86, 107, 110, 135, 150, 161, 175 (both), 176 (bottom), 179 (all), 183, 190, 198, 199, 200 (both), 201.

Wan Meng Hao: pgs 12 (bottom), 13 (both), 14, 15, 17 (top), 24, 25, 33, 36 (bottom), 47 (top), 50, 52 (both), 55 (top), 66, 70 (both), 73 (right), 74, 76, 90–91, 97 (bottom), 99 (bottom), 111 (both), 133 (both), 141, 148 (bottom), 151, 152, 155(bottom), 156–157, 167 (top), 168, 176 (top), 180, 181, 194, 195, 203 (both), 209, 216, 223, 224, 225, 229.

Others:

Lim Chen Sian: pgs 72 (bottom left), 95, 105 (bottom), 192.

Private Collection: pgs 23, 87, 177.

MCIA Archives: pgs 35, 36 (top), 37, 143 (both), 158–159, 169, 206 (both).

ACKNOWLEDGEMENTS

The authors would like to thank the following individuals and institutions for their kind encouragement, patience and assistance: our respective families, Dr Cai Yixiong, Lee Tsen Yang, Lin Yangchen, Marcus Ng, Tony Png, Mrs Lily Tan, Professor Kevin Blackburn, Professor John Miksic, Lim Chen Sian, Omar Chen, Ng Ching Huei, Dr Yeo Kang Shua, Choe Kin Seng, Sng Hock Heng, Miss Yeo Sok Yee, Kelvin Ang Kah Eng, Ms Pauline Phua, Ms G. Uma Devi, Miss Wendy Chan, R. Shankar, Miss Jada Koh, Muhammad Nur Bin Buang, Aaron Lim-Behrend, Tan Sijie, Alex Choo, Benjamin Yap (UBS AG), Hetzel Lelah (Chesed-El Synagogue), Ms Julia Han (Jewish Welfare Board), Gurjeet Singh (Victoria Theatre), Colin Tan (Victoria Concert Hall), Colin Goh (Arts House at the Old Parliament), Ms Toby Huynh (The SGH Museum), Melvin Neo, Shawn Wee, Bernard Go & staff of Marshall Cavendish International (Asia), and friends.